ANYWHERE,
OUT FOR HELP,
AND
THERE A.A.
PONSIBLE.

I am responsible...

When anyone, anywhere,

reaches out for help,

I want the hand of A.A.

always to be there.

And for that: I am responsible.

Alcoholics Anonymous

70 YEARS

of

GROWTH

2005 A.A. International Convention
Toronto, Ontario, Canada
June 30–July 3, 2005

Alcoholics Anonymous

70 YEARS
of
GROWTH

2005 A.A. International Convention
Toronto, Ontario, Canada
June 30–July 3, 2005

Alcoholics Anonymous World Services, Inc.
New York, N.Y.

Photographs and historic materials courtesy of General Service Office Archives, New York.
Material from the A.A. Grapevine is copyrighted by the A.A. Grapevine, Inc.
Reprinted by permission of the publisher.

Grateful acknowledgement is made to: Stepping Stones Foundation; and the many A.A. General Service Offices around the world.

Photo credits, by page number:
14 Silvio Daddi, **21** Peter Stackpole/Getty Images, **23** (bottom) Ken Chaya, **33** Yale University Library, **35** © Bettman/Corbis, **38** (top right) © Royalty-Free/Corbis, **36** Christine Bronico, **47** akg-images, London, **50** (bottom right) Silvio Daddi, **53** (top right) Silvio Daddi, **54** (top left) Silvio Daddi, **59** Paula Bronstein/Getty Images, **62** (bottom left, top right-2) Silvio Daddi, **66** (top right) Silvio Daddi, **71** (top and bottom) Silvio Daddi, **73** John Chard/Getty Images, **76** (top right) Silvio Daddi, **80** (bottom right) Silvio Daddi, **82** Ken Chaya, **83** (bottom right) Silvio Daddi, **85** (bottom right) Ken Chaya.

Book text by Fred DuBose
Book design by Susan Welt

Alcoholics Anonymous World Services, Inc.
Box 459
Grand Central Station
New York, NY 10163

ISBN 1-893007-54-5

Printed in Canada

Contents

A.A. Preamble

Alcoholics Anonymous® is a fellowship of men and women who share their experience, strength and hope with each other that they may solve their common problem and help others to recover from alcoholism.

The only requirement for membership is a desire to stop drinking. There are no dues or fees for A.A. membership; we are self-supporting through our own contributions.

A.A. is not allied with any sect, denomination, politics, organization or institution; does not wish to engage in any controversy; neither endorses nor opposes any causes.

Our primary purpose is to stay sober and help other alcoholics to achieve sobriety.

Welcoming message

Welcome to the 2005 International Convention.

It is again time to celebrate the cherished recovery that this simple program has brought to so many alcoholics around the world.

This International Convention carries the theme "I Am Responsible." All of us know how important it is for the hand of A.A. to always be available to the suffering alcoholic, because members all once reached out for that hand.

We can also celebrate that the hand of A.A. now reaches over 180 countries.

This book gives an overview of the international growth of Alcoholics Anonymous—from the first meeting of two alcoholics in Akron, Ohio, to the now millions around the globe who have recovered from alcoholism.

Of course we are not done yet, our task continues. We all want the hand of A.A. to be there when needed, and each of us can renew our commitment to sharing our experience, strength and hope with the still sick and suffering alcoholic.

So I welcome you to the 2005 International Convention, celebrating 70 years of recovery through Alcoholics Anonymous. Take joy and inspiration from this memorable event, and always remember "I Am Responsible."

Leonard M. Blumenthal, LL.D
Chairperson, General Service Board of Alcoholics Anonymous

Alcoholics Anonymous: The Early Years

A new fellowship of alcoholics struggles to find firm footing, but the idea behind the fledgling movement assures its survival and growth.

They were old pals, both heavy drinkers, and here they sat at a kitchen table in a Brooklyn brownstone in November 1934. Ebby T., at that point sober, had come to Bill W.'s house to talk of his defeat of alcohol with the help of the Oxford Group. Bill had three times gone for treatment at a Manhattan hospital, but still he couldn't stop drinking.

Talk they did on that cold day: about alcohol, about religion, about themselves, and about the Oxford Group, an evangelical movement that counted confession, restitution, and service among its principles. While Bill didn't know it at the time, their afternoon of conversation planted the seed for a movement that would transform lives the world over.

The Return to Towns Hospital

Bill, who had found some success on Wall Street, was out of work and on a binge when Ebby arrived at his door. But Ebby's talk of his former hopelessness, his honesty about his defects, and the power of prayer touched Bill. "In no waking moment," Bill recalled, "could I get that man and his message out of my head."

Feeling low, Bill a few days later decided to investigate the Oxford Group's mission in Manhattan, which was operated through Calvary Church. Though he arrived drunk, he was able to witness to the group of down-and-outers that if Ebby could get help here, he could too. But two or three days of drinking and introspection followed, landing Bill once again in Charles B. Towns Hospital.

During Bill's first visit to Towns in 1933, its director, Dr. William D. Silkworth, explained to him the theory that alcoholism was not a moral defect but an illness—one impossible to defeat by willpower alone. Now, after three failed treatments, a desperate Bill saw nothing ahead but death or madness. Alone in his room, he cried, "If there be a God, let Him show Himself!" Bill later described what happened next: "I was seized with an ecstasy beyond description. . .

Then, seen in the mind's eye, was a mountain. I stood upon its summit. . . Then came the blazing thought, 'You are a free man.'"

When Bill asked whether his experience had been "real," Dr. Silkworth answered, "You are already a different individual. So, my boy, whatever you've got now, you'd better hold onto." Reading William James's *The Varieties of Religious Experience*, brought to the hospital by Ebby, underscored to Bill that his spiritual experience was genuine. In the ensuing days, it dawned on Bill that untold numbers of alcoholics could recover by accepting Dr. Silkworth and Ebby's ideas. He even envisioned a movement of alcoholics helping other alcoholics.

After his release from Towns in mid-December 1934, Bill and his wife Lois began attending meetings of the Oxford Group. (The daughter of a prominent Brooklyn physician, Lois had met Bill when her family summered at Emerald Lake, three miles from Bill's home town of East Dorset, Vermont.) Rev. Dr. Samuel Shoemaker, the rector of Calvary Church and a leading national figure in the Oxford Group, would soon become one of Bill's spiritual advisors and mentors.

In early 1935, Bill began to preach the Oxford message to anyone who would listen.

managed to stop drinking, the very act of talking with them had kept him sober.

Akron, Ohio

In April 1935, Bill traveled to Akron, Ohio, to pursue a business deal that was to go sour.

Dispirited by the failure, Bill was tempted to join in the drinking at the bar in his hotel, the Mayflower. He then realized he needed to talk with another alcoholic. Spotting a roster of local clergymen in the lobby, he picked Rev. William F. Tunks to ring up. That call led to another until he was talking with Henrietta Sieberling, who was trying to aid an alcoholic physician in the Oxford Group. His name was Robert S., and he, a Vermonter like Bill, was to become known to the Fellowship as Dr. Bob.

With the stage set for the two men to meet, the doctor and his wife, Anne, arrived at Henrietta's home on May 15 at five o'clock. Bob had told his wife he planned to stay for no more than 15 minutes. "After dinner, which Bob did not eat," Bill recalled, "Henrietta discreetly put us off in her little library. There, Bob and I talked until after eleven o'clock." As two Vermonters and alcoholics, the men spoke the same language, and Bob was intrigued to learn of Dr. Silkworth's view of alcoholism as an illness.

Bill decided to extend his stay in Akron and began visiting Dr. Bob and Anne for morning "guidance sessions," an Oxford practice revolving around Bible readings, and soon

East Dorset, Vermont. *Bill W. was born on November 26, 1895 in East Dorset and was raised in the corner house shown above. The family was split when Bill's father left home in 1905 and Bill's mother decided to study medicine in Boston. Bill and younger sister Dorothy moved in with their maternal grandparents.*

He also spent long hours at Calvary Mission and at Towns, where Dr. Silkworth permitted him to talk with some of the patients. But after six months, none of the men had sobered up. Dr. Silkworth identified Bill's preaching as one of the causes, advising him to "get out of the driver's seat" and talk instead about the illness of alcoholism before "trying out. . . the ethical principles [of] the Oxford Group." Lois reminded Bill that even though none of his prospects had

9

Which name to choose? *Why Bill picked the name of Rev. William F. Tunks (left) from the roster in the lobby of Akron's Mayflower Hotel isn't known—but Bill later called it a "ten strike" because the Reverend instantly told him of ten people (most affiliated with the Oxford Group) who might lead him to an alcoholic to talk with.*

moved to their house. The three also attended weekly Oxford Group meetings.

The date of Dr. Bob's last drink—June 10, 1935, after one last binge—is marked as the day A.A. was born. From then on, he and Bill wasted no time in searching out alcoholics, spending hours figuring out the most effective ways to reach them. They agreed that while an alcoholic can't be told what to do, another drunk sharing his own story could reach even the worst cases. They also realized that because no alcoholic wants to face life without drinking, thinking of sobriety in small chunks of time makes it more bearable. "One day at a time," they put it, arriving at the twenty-four hour concept. They also scored a success: Bill D., an Akron City Hospital patient, became the third member of a budding fellowship.

In late August 1935, Bill returned home. Almost two and a half years would pass before he and Dr. Bob would again meet face-to-face. In the interim, Bill sought out alcoholics at Towns Hospital, where he met Henry "Hank" P., an energetic salesman who had lost a plum job with a major oil company because of his drinking. Bill also began to hold meetings at his home at 182 Clinton Street in Brooklyn as he continued working with alcoholics through the Oxford Group.

Despite Bill's solid relationship with Rev. Dr. Shoemaker, tension began to build between the Oxford Group at Calvary Church and Bill's band of struggling alcoholics (members of the former describing the latter's meetings as "narrow and divisive"), prompting Bill and Lois's exit from the organization in 1937.

Later that year, Bill visited Dr. Bob in Akron. Taking stock, they were amazed to come up with 35, possibly 40 men who had gotten sober. For the first time they saw, as Bill said, "that this thing was going to succeed." Fired with visions of books on alcoholism, a chain of hospitals for alcoholics, and missionaries carrying the message, Bill saw another need as well: the funds to make it happen.

The Quest for Support

Bill and Dr. Bob (who liked the book idea but had reservations about the missionaries and hospitals, feeling they could harm the spirit of the movement) then presented the proposals to the Akron members. Though many members felt that paid workers would kill goodwill and that hospitals might make the movement look like a

Home base in Manhattan. *Calvary Church, on East 21st Street at Gramercy Park, became Bill's Manhattan base of operations on his return from Akron. He often stayed overnight at Calvary House (an eight-story building behind the church) and met with alcoholics from the nearby Calvary Mission.*

racket, a vote for all three proposals passed— but just barely. Raising money to fund such efforts, however, would fall to Bill.

Back in New York, Bill received enthusiastic support from the group but no interest from potential investors. In the fall of 1937, a down-hearted Bill sought advice from his brother-in-law, Dr. Leonard Strong, Jr. Leonard, it so happened, was acquainted with Willard

Richardson, connected with the Rockefeller philanthropies (John D. Rockefeller, Jr. had been a champion of Prohibition). Leonard telephoned Richardson, who agreed to meet with Bill the following day.

Thus began a series of meetings—with the next held in Rockefeller's board room—where it was agreed that large-scale funding of the Fellowship could compromise its purpose. Recognition of the need for some kind of structure to guide the movement and oversee its funds led to the establishment of the Alcoholic Foundation. (See "Four Early Friends," page 12.)

The All-Important Book

In the spring of 1938 Bill began work on the book that was to become the main text of the Fellowship. After the first two chapters were completed, he showed them to Harper & Brothers, which offered to publish the book when it was finished. But Bill hesitated. He wondered if it was wise to let an outside publisher own what might become an important part of the new society. Most of the trustees, however, were delighted over the publisher's offer. Bill expressed his misgivings, and a meeting called to consider the subject ended in a hung vote.

Enter Henry "Hank" P., the "salesman's salesman" with whom Bill was working in Newark. Bill and most of the other members agreed to Hank's plan to form a publishing company and sell shares in it for $25 each. Sales of the stock,

Four Early Friends

Joining Bill W., Dr. Bob, Dr. Silkworth, and others at the December 1937 meeting held in John D. Rockefeller, Jr.'s private boardroom were four nonalcoholics, each of whom would go on to do his part to support the new Fellowship. Willard Richardson and Frank Amos became two of the three nonalcoholic members of the Alcoholic Foundation's first board of trustees.

Willard Richardson, *who was connected with the Rockefeller philanthropies, was the man who called the meeting after being introduced to Bill W. Bill later wrote of Richardson, "[His] steady faith, wisdom, and spiritual quality were our main anchors to windward during the squalls that fell on A.A. and its embryo service center in the first years."*

Albert Scott, *head of an engineering firm and Chairman of the Board of Trustees of Riverside Church in Manhattan, presided at the 1937 meeting. It was he who posed the question about the Fellowship that, as Bill later wrote in* Alcoholics Anonymous Comes of Age, *"is still heard in A.A. to this day: 'Won't money spoil this thing?'"*

Frank Amos, *an advertising executive, visited Akron and subsequently caught Rockefeller's attention with a glowing report of the activities of Dr. Bob and Akron's first group. Amos also encouraged the formation of the Alcoholic Foundation.*

A. LeRoy Chipman *was a Rockefeller associate who went on to serve for many years as treasurer of the Alcoholic Foundation. He also raised most of the money needed to pay off the shareholders of Works Publishing, Inc., which resulted in the Foundation's sole ownership of the Big Book.*

however, went nowhere.

A *Reader's Digest* editor whom Bill and Hank approached expressed interest in the book and made what sounded like a promise to carry a story when it was published. Based on this exciting development, A.A. members and friends began to invest.

But things would not work out as planned: While the book—titled *Alcoholics Anonymous*—did indeed roll off the presses, the *Reader's Digest* article fell through. As a result, the books virtually sat idle in the warehouse, the beginning of two years of minimal sales.

Even a good review in the *New York Times* failed to generate interest. Before the broadcast of a radio interview of Morgan R., who spoke of the book and his recovery through A.A. on the popular radio show "We the People," Hank mailed order cards to thousands of physicians—yet only two book orders came in. During this time, Bill and Lois lost their Clinton Street home and had no choice but to live first with one A.A. family, then another.

In 1939 came two successes: An article in the *Cleveland Plain Dealer* caused membership to surge in that city, and Charles Towns succeeded in getting an article on A.A. into *Liberty* magazine. And 17 months later came the story that changed everything: Jack Alexander's "Alcoholics Anonymous," the lead article in the March 1, 1941 *Saturday Evening Post*.

The impact was immediate, with some A.A. groups doubling in size scarcely a week after the article was published. Even more dramatic was the deluge of letters and book orders. In the article's wake, A.A. groups began to form beyond New York and Ohio, spreading to Toronto and Windsor in Canada and all the way to Honolulu. By 1944, the Fellowship was well-established, with an estimated 10,000 members.

The Shift in Authority

By spring 1948, Bill knew that the survival of A.A. headquarters (see page 29) and board required involving A.A. groups more directly. A lengthy trip to talk with A.A.s all across the U.S. and Canada convinced him that A.A. members felt the same way. He suggested to Dr. Bob that the groups be officially linked to the board and headquarters by a "conference" made up of elected delegates from the groups.

However, with the exception of chairman Bernard Smith, who was to become the chief architect of the General Service Conference structure, the trustees were satisfied with the status quo, as were many old-timers in New York, Akron, Cleveland, and Chicago. Dr. Bob, too, had his reservations, suggesting in a letter to Bill that "for the moment, perhaps, 'easy does it' is the best course to follow.'"

Shortly before he died, Dr. Bob consented to having the Conference, and Bernard Smith finally convinced the board to back it. It then fell to Bill to work out the details. His plan called for each state and province to have one delegate, though those with large A.A. populations could have more. The delegates would be divided into two panels serving for two years, each elected every other year for the sake of continuity. As for the issue of authority, with a two-thirds vote the delegates could issue "flat directives" to the trustees.

In April 1951, the First General Service Conference met in New York City. (Today it consists of area delegates who account for at least two-thirds of the Conference body, trustees, directors of A.A. World Services and the Grapevine, and A.A. staff members of the General Service Office and the Grapevine.)

The culmination of the Fellowship's early years came at the historic 1955 International Convention in St. Louis, by which time Alcoholics Anonymous was active in more than two dozen countries. It was here that Bill officially handed the leadership over to the members. The society that he and Dr. Bob had sought to make a reality 20 years before would now begin a half-century more of growth.

The Twelve Traditions

In the three years following the publication of the *Saturday Evening Post* article, much of the office work at New York headquarters consisted of answering letters asking for help to start new groups or requesting advice for solving a group's problems. Each letter required a personal response, and Bill wrote many of them himself. Seeing similar questions arise over and over—and hearing long-time members' talk of the need for clear guidance for A.A. groups and individuals—Bill set about devising guidelines in late 1945.

Rather than calling the guidelines "rules" or "regulations," he chose "traditions"—a word that captured the A.A. spirit. A tradition on anonymity was already in place. Others, including a tradition against expressing opinions on issues outside the society, were new. The Traditions, which numbered twelve, were first published in the April 1946 issue of the A.A. Grapevine. Bill then wrote an article on each for later issues of the magazine, explaining each Tradition's origin.

The Big Book

Cornerstone of the Fellowship's literature, Alcoholics Anonymous *was born of the efforts of many.*

When Bill W. and Dr. Bob realized in 1937 that their budding fellowship of alcoholics had the potential for real growth, they reflected on the need for a book that would crystallize the message. In a talk Bill gave in Fort Worth, Texas, in June 1954, he recalled the impetus:

"Up to this moment, not a syllable of this program was in writing. It was a kind of word-of-mouth deal, with variations according to each man's or woman's standing. In a general way, we'd say to a new prospect: 'Well, the booze has got you down, and you've got an allergy and an obsession and you're hopeless. You'd better get honest with yourself and take stock; you ought to talk this out with somebody, kind of a confessional, and you ought to make restitution for the harms you did. Then you pray as best you can, according to your likes.' Now that was the sum of the word-of-mouth program up to that time.

"How could we unify this thing? Could we, out of our experience, describe certain methods that had done the trick for us? Obviously, if this movement was to propagate, it had to have liter-ature so its message would not be garbled, either by the drunk or by the general public."

As it turned out, approximately a hundred early A.A. members would contribute in one way or another to the creation of the book that would come to be titled *Alcoholics Anonymous.* The story of how Bill W. paced the floor of Hank P.'s office in Newark, New Jersey, dictating chapters to secretary Ruth Hock is well known, but each chapter was not only the result of an outline based on hours of discussion with members but was also subjected to their review. Bill read finished drafts to the New York group at its weekly meetings. He also sent copies to Dr. Bob to share with the Akronites, who generally made favorable comments. The New York members, though, gave the chapters, in Bill's words, "a real mauling." "I redictated them," he said, "and Ruth retyped them over and over."

Twelve Steps, Many Stories

Work continued, and it soon came time for Bill to write the chapter that would explain how the

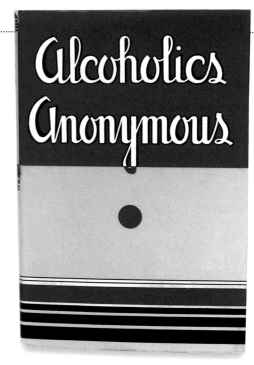

First Edition. *The earliest Big Books sported a red and yellow "circus cover."*

program of recovery actually worked. The basic concept of the program revolved around six Oxford Group-inspired precepts. Bill slowly realized they should be broken up into smaller pieces to close any loopholes through which, in his words, "a rationalizing alcoholic could wiggle out." Suddenly inspired, he took little more than a half hour to finish the first draft. When he numbered the new steps, there were twelve.

New York and Akron members who reviewed the steps gave them mixed reviews, with some objecting to the use of the word "God." Yet Bill saw this as a positive. The society's group conscience was at work, he reasoned, to construct the best book possible. In the end, "God" was modified to "God as we understood Him."

It also became clear that the book needed to recount the personal experiences of sober alcoholics. Dr. Bob and the Akronites were leaders in this effort. Jim, a former newspaperman with two years of sobriety, interviewed and wrote the stories of the Ohio members who had solid sobriety records. (Dr. Bob wrote his own.) In New York, the members wrote their own stories, which Bill and Hank then edited.

Bill later described the story section as "our principal means of identifying with readers outside A.A.; it is the written equivalent of hearing speakers at an A.A. meeting."

The book was completed in January 1939. A final edit was done by a faculty member at New York University, after which Bill and Hank took the manuscript to Cornwall Press, the printer. The retail price was set at $3.50, and the presses would roll after the sympathetic printer accepted a small down payment of $500 for a run of 5,000 copies.

What's in a Name?

Earlier, 400 copies of the pre-publication manuscript had been mailed out to various A.A. members and friends of A.A., each bearing the title *Alcoholics Anonymous.*

For months the Akron and New York groups had been voting on various titles, and "Alcoholics Anonymous" was among the earliest suggested. But it was unpopular with many. "The Way Out" was favored by a considerable majority, and it would have won the contest had a check of the Library of Congress not turned up 12 books of the same name.

So it happened that the book got its title and the new society its name. And "Big Book?" The nickname came from the finished product's bulkiness, the result of instructions to the printer to use his thickest paper stock so that readers would feel they were "getting their money's worth."

A deal at any price. *The original price of the Big Book was $3.50, and the hardcover Fourth Edition went on sale 62 years later for only $1.50 more. Today* Alcoholics Anonymous *is published in more than 50 languages and is available in hardcover, paperback, audiotape, Braille, and filmed sign language editions.*

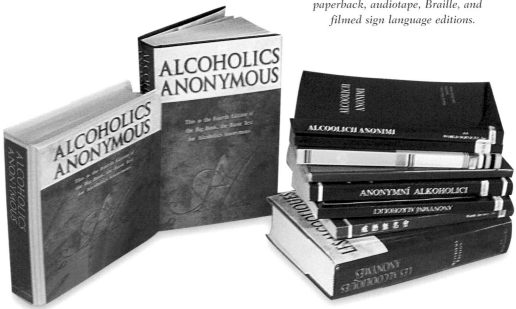

The Grapevine

The monthly magazine that began on a wing and a prayer has been going strong for 61 years.

In the spring of 1944, six New York A.A. members (four women, two men) decided to start a newsletter for New York City A.A.s. They then took their idea to Bill W., who noted that A.A. would need a national magazine some day, and maybe the time had come. He encouraged them to give it a try.

Collecting articles, borrowing money to pay for paper and printing, and working out of their apartments, the editors brought out the first issue of the Grapevine in June 1944, with a print run of 1,200 copies priced at 15 cents. The editors sent complimentary copies of the first issue to the secretaries of all listed groups and to all known A.A. members in the armed forces, including those fighting in what was to become World War II's final year. The soldiers began calling the magazine their "meeting in print," a description that quickly became universal.

The magazine's most prolific contributor was Bill W., who often spoke of it as a "mirror of the Fellowship" and a "forum for debate." He put into his Grapevine articles his thoughts on vital A.A. issues. In the 1940s Bill used the magazine to set forth and then elaborate on the Twelve Traditions, and in later issues would introduce the controversial idea of a General Service Conference structure.

Change and Growth

As the years passed, news articles and contributors' submissions gradually shifted from past drinking to current sobriety. By 1974, international circulation had topped 72,000 and was climbing. Four years later, circulation reached 100,000. Unlike traditional magazines, the A.A. Grapevine neither promotes itself nor accepts advertising, and its contributors, who are unpaid, come from the ranks of the Fellowship.

"Meetings in print" in many languages. *Among the international equivalents of the Grapevine are* Partage *(published in Brussels and serving Belgium, France, and Luxembourg);* De Boei *from the Netherlands;* Zdroj *from Poland; and* Akron–1935 *from Spain, the title of which memorializes the beginnings of Alcoholics Anonymous in a city far across the sea.*

By the mid 1980s, selected articles from the magazine that Bill once attributed to the efforts of six "ink-stained wretches" were available on audiotape. Milestones were reached in 1996, when *La Viña* (the bimonthly Spanish-language edition) was published, and in 2004, when the Grapevine Digital Archive was launched.

Additional A.A. Literature

As A.A. spread around the globe, its books and pamphlets were translated and overseas offices began to publish their own literature.

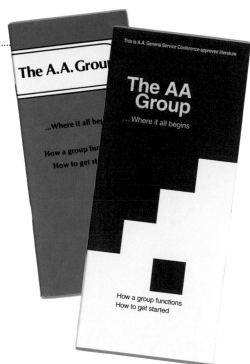

A new look.
In 1989, the design of A.A. pamphlets was made more up-to-date.

The publication in 1939 of the Fellowship's main text, *Alcoholics Anonymous,* was followed by the first pamphlet (with the equally simple title of *A.A.*) in April 1940. In it were seven articles on A.A. recently written by a newspaper reporter (and A.A. member) and published in his paper, the *Houston Press;* also included was Dr. Harry Emerson Fosdick's review of the Big Book. From those beginnings has grown a large inventory of recovery literature, printed matter for professionals, directories, and A.A. service material produced by A.A. World Services, Inc. (AAWS) and general service offices worldwide.

A Multilingual Endeavor

The need for translations of its literature also grew, and translators in Quebec were pioneers in this regard, making literature available in French. Among Europe's first versions of the Big Book—now available in more than 50 languages—were those in Norwegian and German. Pamphlets produced in New York for distribution in the U.S. and Canada also began to be translated, reaching alcoholics in Europe, Asia, Africa, and the Spanish-speaking world.

As service structures were established overseas and general service offices opened, many became able to handle not only their own translations but also the production of A.A. literature. Then, as now, the first step a foreign office took was asking permission of A.A.W.S. The process involves submitting for approval a sample of the translation of the desired publication; once approval has been granted, A.A. offices are licensed to produce and distribute the publication. Today, various A.A. pamphlets, directories, handbooks, and the Fellowship's mainstay books (including *Alcoholics Anonymous Comes of Age,* *"Pass It On"*, and *Dr. Bob and the Good Oldtimers*), other literature, and audio-visual material are produced in some 70 languages.

In addition, A.A. members worldwide have benefited from the new technology. It was only to be expected that when the G.S.O. New York-designed website (www.aa.org) went online in 1991 that information would be accessible in English, Spanish, and French. Today general service offices on five continents maintain their own Web sites, meaning that A.A. literature can be read online virtually anywhere. The Fellowship's earliest members would no doubt be pleased to learn that A.A. literature is not limited to printed matter but is available in multiple other formats as well.

70 YEARS *of* GROWTH

19 35 — 20 04

". . . the thought came that there were thousands of hopeless

alcoholics who might be glad to have what had been so freely

given me. Perhaps I could help some of them. They in turn

might work with others."

— From "Bill's Story" (*Alcoholics Anonymous*)

1935—1944

A fellowship like no other

An alcoholic from New York has a vision of the way to sobriety and is introduced to a like-minded doctor from Akron. Their first meeting will lead to the creation of a Twelve Step recovery program and a book that will change the lives of millions. In Alcoholic Anonymous's first decade, there is no setback that cannot be overcome by the power of Bill W. and Dr. Bob's idea.

Joining the fold...
Canada

World War II sailor on leave

Bill and Lois join the Oxford Group

Following Bill W.'s spiritual awakening at Towns Hospital (late 1934), he and wife Lois join the Oxford Group—a nondenominational movement whose tenets are based on the "Four Absolutes" of honesty, purity, unselfishness, and love—and begin to attend meetings at Calvary House, behind Manhattan's Calvary Episcopal Church.

Bill is inspired by the charismatic rector Rev. Dr. Samuel Shoemaker (above), who emphasizes one-on-one sharing and guidance.

A business trip to Akron

A short-term job opportunity takes Bill to Akron, Ohio. In the lobby of his hotel, he finds himself fighting the urge to join in the conviviality in the bar. He consults a church directory posted on the wall with the aim of finding someone who might lead him to an alcoholic with whom he could talk. A phone call to the Episcopal minister Rev. William Tunks results in a referral to Henrietta Seiberling, a committed Oxford Group adherent who has tried for two years to bring a fellow group member, a prominent Akron surgeon, to sobriety.

GREETINGS *from* AKRON OHIO
RUBBER MANUFACTURING CENTER OF THE WORLD

1935–36

Bill's group within a group

Bill is asked to speak at a large Oxford Group meeting at Calvary House. His subject is alcoholism, and after the meeting Bill is approached by a man who says he desperately wants to get sober. He becomes the first of a group of alcoholics from the Oxford Group and Calvary Mission who meet with Bill at nearby Stewart's Cafeteria. Though none of these men achieve lasting sobriety, Bill's ability to reach alcoholics grows after he seeks counsel from Dr. Robert Silkworth of Towns Hospital, who suggests he do less preaching and speak more about alcoholism as an illness.

The meeting at the gatehouse

Henrietta Seiberling, daughter-in-law of the founder of the Goodyear Rubber Company, invites Bill to the Seiberling estate, where she lives in the gatehouse (below). She tells him of the struggle of Dr. Robert S., and the meeting of the two men takes place the next day—Mother's Day, 1935. In the privacy of the library, Bill spills out his story, inspiring "Dr. Bob," as Henrietta calls him, to share his own. As the meeting ends hours later, Dr. Bob comes to realize that spiritual support is the result of one alcoholic talking to another alcoholic.

Forging friendships in Akron
After Seiberling secures a room for Bill at the nearby Portage Country Club, he joins the Smiths at the weekly Oxford Group meetings held in the home of T. Henry Williams and his wife Clarace, both particularly sympathetic to the plight of alcoholics. At the suggestion of Dr. Bob's wife Anne, Bill soon moves to their home at 855 Ardmore Avenue (below).

Men on a mission
After Dr. Bob lapses into drinking again but quickly recovers, he and Bill spend hours working out the best approach to alcoholics, a group known to be averse to taking directions. Realizing that thinking of sobriety for a day at a time makes it seem more achievable than facing a lifetime of struggle, they hit on the twenty-four hour concept.

Bill's return to New York
Bill takes the train home to New York to seek a job, but his need to help other alcoholics is no less urgent. He begins to look for prospects at Towns Hospital, where he finds Hank P., a driven businessman who becomes his first success from Towns. Another success is Fitz M., a Southerner and the son of a minister. Both become Bill's close friends and allies.

"The man on the bed"
Eager to carry the message, Bill and Dr. Bob search for another person to help. After a slow start, their call to Akron City Hospital yields a prospect—Bill

D., a lawyer. During the visits of Bill and Dr. Bob, Bill D. takes their message to heart and promises never to drink again—a vow he keeps for life. Now remembered as the "first man on the bed" (above, as depicted in a painting by an A.A. member), Bill D. becomes the third member of what will eventually be called Alcoholics Anonymous.

The office that will go down in A.A. history
Bill begins to commute to a small office at 17 William Street, Newark, New Jersey (right), joining Hank P. to raise money for a new busi-

ness venture—Honor Dealers, an attempt to create a cooperative program for gasoline dealers in northern New Jersey. The office secretary is a young woman named Ruth Hock.

Weekly meetings at 182 Clinton
In an effort to strengthen his prospects' chances for recovery, Bill welcomes them to his home at 182 Clinton Street in Brooklyn. The Tuesday night meetings soon give way to temporary residency for some participants—the kind of "way station" arrangement that Dr. Bob and his wife Anne have pioneered in Akron.

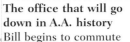

An offer spurs "group conscience"

Charles B. Towns, owner of Towns Hospital (below), suggests that Bill move his work to the hospital to treat alcoholics, conduct his meetings, and share in the establishment's profits. At the Clinton Street meeting that very evening, Bill tells his group of the offer—but the members object, insisting that spreading the message for money would violate its integrity. Bill will later see this resistance to commercialism as a first example of what he called group conscience— the wisdom of the group over that of individual leaders. Below: Bill's first admission slip to Towns.

Plans for the future

In late 1937, Bill pays another visit to Dr. Bob in Akron. Comparing notes, they are astonished to find that at least 40 of the many alcoholics with whom they've worked have stayed sober for two years. This discovery leads to discussions of the possibility of a chain of hospitals for the treatment of alcoholics, paid missionaries who would spread the word, and literature—especially a book meant to carry the message far and wide.

1937–38

Action in Akron

Oxford Group meetings for alcoholics continue at the large home of T. Henry and Clarace Williams (below), with Dr. Bob sometimes joining Mr. Williams to lead meetings. The recovering alcoholics of the group refer to themselves as the "alcoholic squadron of the Oxford Group."

A momentous meeting

Bill's attempts to raise money prove unsuccessful. In 1937, his brother-in-law, Dr. Leonard Strong, Jr., is able to set up a session with men connected to the philanthropies headed by John D. Rockefeller, Jr. (above). At a December meeting attended by Bill, Dr. Bob, Dr. Silkworth, and a few group members from New York and Akron, the potential backers are moved and impressed by the Fellowship's work. However, after it is pointed out that money could spoil the mission, the meeting reaps welcome enthusiasm and moral support, but no funds.

CHARLES B. TOWNS HOSPITAL
293 Central Park West
New York 24, N.Y.

24

Rockefeller's stance

Frank Amos (below), who attended the December meeting and is a close friend of John D. Rockefeller, Jr., agrees to assess the Akron group and explore the possibility of opening a small hospital for alcoholics. In February, 1938 he spends several days in the city. Impressed by the recovery rate of Akron group members, he proposes a recuperating facility to be run by Dr. Bob. To Rockefeller he recommends a sum of $50,000 for the early work, but Rockefeller thinks the Fellowship should be self-supporting. The philanthropist does, however, contribute $5,000 toward Bill and Dr. Bob's basic needs.

The Alcoholic Foundation

Frank Amos and others who had attended the December meeting offer to confer with Bill, Leonard Strong, and various members of the New York group to consider how the movement can be given an organizational framework. As a result, the Alcoholic Foundation is formally established on August 11, 1938, with Dr. Bob as a trustee and Bill on the advisory committee.

The Twelve Steps

As he writes, Bill comes to the point where he must outline an actual program for the recovering alcoholic to follow. Drawing on the teachings of Sam Shoemaker, William James's *The Varieties of Religious Experience*, and the Oxford Group-inspired six-step procedure used by Bill and Dr. Bob as they carry the message, Bill incorporates the theme of hope into the steps. The steps grow to 12, and the A.A. Twelve Step program is born.

The Big Book gets started

Bill begins to write the book meant to aid the alcoholic who is unable to attend meetings or find fellow alcoholics with whom to talk. At the Newark office, he dictates his handwritten notes to Ruth Hock (right) as she types, reviewing and revising drafts all the while. These chapters are mimeographed and mailed to potential financial backers, as well as to Eugene Exman, the religion editor at Harper & Brothers publishers.

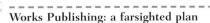

Works Publishing: a farsighted plan

Harper & Brothers offers to publish the Big Book, much to the delight of Bill and the trustees. But farsighted businessman Hank P. convinces Bill to sell shares in their own company and to publish the volume themselves. Hank works up a prospectus for what will become Works Publishing Company, with 600 shares of stock selling at $25 per share (right).

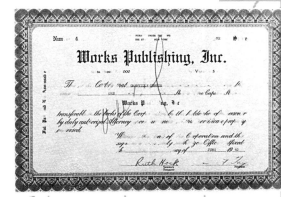

The Big Book tests the waters

Four hundred mimeographed copies of the Big Book manuscript are sent out for comments and evaluation by members, friends, and other allies. Among those making valuable contributions are a Baltimore doctor who suggests having a physician write the introduction (a job taken on by Dr. Silkworth) and Dr. Harry Emerson Fosdick (above), the highly respected minister of Manhattan's Riverside Church, who warmly approves of the book and responds with a positive review to be used as the Fellowship wishes.

An offshoot—and new name—in Cleveland

Clarence S., a Cleveland resident who attends Oxford Group meetings in Akron, announces that he and other Clevelanders will be starting a group open only to alcoholics and their families. Like some other breakaway groups, they will also adopt the name of the Big Book mimeographs now circulating in Akron—"Alcoholics Anonymous." In May 1939, the first A.A. meeting in Cleveland is held in the home of Al G. (also known as Abby G.), a patent lawyer.

Main Avenue Bridge, Cleveland

1939

Publication and disappointment

In March 1939, some 5,000 copies of the Big Book—titled *Alcoholics Anonymous*—roll off the press. After an anticipated *Reader's Digest* article fails to materialize and a radio broadcast reaps no orders, sales are few and far between. This disappointment foreshadows a bleak summer for the New York fellowship.

Bill and Lois lose 182 Clinton Street

As the Great Depression eases and property values rise, the company that owns the mortgage on 182 Clinton Street (right) sells the building, forcing Bill and Lois to move out. Thus begins the couple's two years of temporary residency in the homes of Hank P. and other A.A. families, with Bill and Lois carrying the program's message for the duration of this unsettled period.

Dr. Bob serves with Sister Ignatia
In the spring of 1939, Dr. Bob suggests to Sister Ignatia Gavin (right), with whom he had worked at Akron's St. Thomas hospital (above) since 1934, that they start treating alcoholics. She agrees, and over the years Sister Ignatia and Dr. Bob will bring comfort and aid to almost 5,000 hospitalized patients.

A first for women
After reading the Big Book while a sanitarium patient in Greenwich, Connecticut, Marty M. starts attending meetings at 182 Clinton Street. She will become the first woman in Alcoholics Anonymous to achieve lasting sobriety.

The dawn of sponsorship
Sponsorship—the sharing of an A.A.'s personal experiences with other alcoholics trying to achieve sobriety—grows out of the awareness that loyalty is owed to the A.A. program itself, not individuals. Contributing to sponsorship is the rapid growth and differing viewpoints of groups in Cleveland, where the idea of rotating leadership every six months is developed. Rotation is seen as a way of bolstering identification with the larger program—and, in kind, the concept of sponsorship.

A highly effective tool
In an effort to create a lifeline, all A.A. members in Akron write their names in small address books that are then presented to newcomers. In the words of an early member, "They'd say, 'Put a nickel in that telephone and call before you take a drink. If nobody answers, call somebody else." Such "telephone therapy" grows to become an effective instrument of sobriety and a major facilitator of sponsorship.

A lift from *Liberty*
Seeking publicity for A.A., Charles Towns recounts its history to writer Morris Markey, who will submit the article "Alcoholics and God" (a title with which Bill isn't comfortable) to Fulton Oursler, editor of the popular weekly *Liberty*. After the article's publication on September 30, 1939, sales of the Big Book increase by several hundred and the Newark office receives 800 pleas for help from alcoholics and their loved ones.

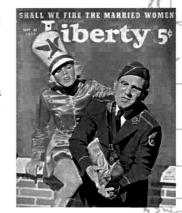

Another split from the Oxford Group
In the fall, tensions grow in the Akron Oxford Group, with the alcoholic members wanting more independence. The alcoholics decide to meet at Dr. Bob's home, though Bob remains loyal to T. Henry and Clarace Williams. As this fledgling group grows, it shifts its meetings to King School.

The first New York clubhouse
With 182 Clinton no longer available for meetings, New York members meet wherever they can. Two of them, Bert T. and Horace C., find and guarantee the rent on a small building at 334½ West 24th Street in Manhattan. The clubhouse (right) soon bustles with activity, and Bill and Lois move into one of the two upstairs bedrooms later in the year.

1940

Rockefeller's dinner
John D. Rockefeller, Jr. hosts a dinner at the exclusive Union Club (above) to publicize Alcoholics Anonymous. Because Rockefeller's belief that A.A. should be self-supporting is understood by the guests, no money is solicited or raised. Nevertheless, Rockefeller sees to it that the event receives favorable and widespread publicity. Within a month, small donations trickle in from members, slightly easing the financial burden.

Lightening up
At meetings, Bill and other A.A. members employ humor and self-deprecation when telling of their harrowing personal experiences. The humor is sometimes black, but always empathetic. In later writings,

Bill states that his intent is not to deny the truth or soften reality of the alcoholic's experience, but to make it easier to share by softening its terrible sting.

A challenge to the principle of anonymity

A star catcher for the Cleveland Indians, described by the press as "rollicking" because of his heavy drinking, announces that he has achieved sobriety through his year-long membership in Alcoholics Anonymous. His name and face are splashed over sports pages nationwide. Such violation of the Fellowship's principle of anonymity leads Bill and members everywhere to consider anonymity's pros and cons.

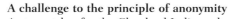

A.A.'s first headquarters

In March, Works Publishing moves from Newark to a small office at 30 Vesey Street (below) in lower Manhattan. Though something of a financial gamble, the move means that for the first time the Fellowship has a head-quarters of its own.

Enter Father Dowling

On a rainy winter night in late 1940, a kindly clergyman from St. Louis appears at the 24th Street Clubhouse. Leaning on his cane, Fr. Edward Dowling, SJ, (right) introduces himself to Bill, states that he has been reading *Alcoholics Anonymou*s, and then points out the parallels between the Twelve Steps and his own Jesuit order. Thus begins a spiritual sponsorship that will last for the next 20 years.

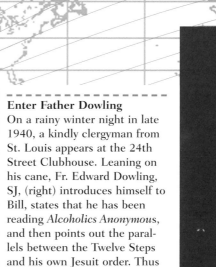

A.A. marches west

A.A. spreads beyond Ohio, with groups beginning to meet in cities as large as Chicago and New Orleans and Houston. Alcoholics in Topeka, Fort Worth, Tucson, Omaha, and Honolulu also "join the club," as do those in smaller towns in the Midwest and West.

The *Saturday Evening Post* makes history

The interest of Judge Curtis Bok, owner and publisher of *The Saturday Evening Post,* is piqued when he learns of A.A. from two Philadelphia friends. Bok then calls on hard-nosed reporter Jack Alexander to tell the organization's story. The resulting 7,500-word article is published in the magazine on March 1, 1941, putting Alcoholics Anonymous on the map of public consciousness and spurring a dramatic increase in Big Book sales and membership alike.

1941–42

Toronto gets the message

The Fellowship's message will spread north when Rev. Dr. George Little (far right), a Toronto United Church minister who is also active in the temperance movement, learns of the Big Book in 1940, orders a few copies, and gives two to a small group of alcoholics who have been gathering for mutual support. Led by Tom E., the men will become Canada's first A.A. group as they begin to hold meetings in a room above Toronto's Little Denmark Tavern in 1943 (right).

The first special interest group

The first all-women group is founded in Cleveland in 1941, making it A.A.'s inaugural special interest group. Women in New York, Minneapolis, Salt Lake City, and San Diego soon follow suit, and by the mid 1940s the ratio of women to men in the A.A. population is roughly one in six. Women's groups light the way for other special interest groups, which will eventually include those for young people, the elderly, gays and lesbians, and doctors, lawyers, and other professionals.

Bill and Lois move to Bedford Hills

Friends in Westchester County, a half-hour north of New York City, help Bill and Lois work out a financial plan that enables them to acquire a house in Bedford Hills. On April 11, 1941, the couple spend their first night there. The comfortable shingled, hip-roofed house (right), which they will name Stepping Stones, affords them a measure of privacy for the first time since Alcoholics Anonymous was founded.

A.A.'s first prison group

A campaign for prison reform by Clinton T. Duffy, warden of San Quentin Prison in San Francisco, calls for addressing the special needs of inmates who had been drinking when committing a crime. Duffy seeks aid and advice from California A.A. members, leading to the formation of a prison group at San Quentin. The inmates hold their first meeting in 1942.

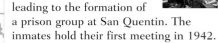

Bill hits the road

Membership reaches some 2,000 in March 1941, and by November has jumped to approximately 6,000 members in 200 groups across the country. Bill begins what will be three years of traveling to visit groups, getting to know many members individually.

A letter from Australia

After reading an article on Alcoholics Anonymous in the *American Journal of Psychiatry*, Dr. Sylvester Minogue (left), the medical superintendent of Rydalmere Hospital in Sydney, writes a letter to the Alcoholic Foundation in New York. His request for information results in his receipt of the Big Book and continuing correspondence with secretary Bobbie B. of the New York office, setting the stage for the start-up of A.A. groups in Australia.

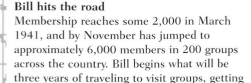

31

1943–44

Canada's second group forms in Windsor

In October, 1943, a second Canadian group gets off the ground when alcoholics begin to meet in Windsor, Ontario.

The Grapevine debuts

An eight-page bulletin intended to get A.A. news to members (including soldiers overseas) expands to become the Fellowship's official magazine, with the first issue published in June 1944.
It comes to be called "a meeting in print."

Bill keeps traveling

As group after group sprouts up, Bill continues traveling around the country, often accompanied by Lois. His arrival in towns large and small is cause for great excitement as A.A. members flock to hear his talks and speak with him one-on-one. The announcement shown at right invites people to hear Bill speak at an open meeting in Connecticut.

The Hartford Group
of
ALCOHOLICS ANONYMOUS
Cordially invite you to attend an
OPEN MEETING
on
TUESDAY, FEBRUARY 2ND, 1943, AT 8:15 P. M.
WILLIAM "BILL" W., CO-FOUNDER
will talk on
"ALCOHOLICS ANONYMOUS *and the* ALCOHOLIC PROBLEM"

WEST MIDDLE SCHOOL AUDITORIUM 927 Asylum Avenue, Hartford, Conn.	·A·A· P. O. Box 592 Hartford, Conn.	*Guest Speakers* BILL WILSON, Co-Founder A HARTFORD JUDGE AN OUTSTANDING WOMAN AA A CATHOLIC PRIEST A CLERGYMAN REPRESENTATIVES OF THE GROUP

The GRAPEVINE

VOL. I, NO. 1, JUNE, 1944 P. O. BOX 328, GRAND CENTRAL ANNEX YEARLY SUBSCRIPTION, 1.50; COPY, 15c

May we remind those who see, read and possess a copy of this paper but who are not members of A.A. of the meaning of those two initials . . and ask them to respect our anonymity? Please do not quote or reprint without our permission.

TWO YALE SAVANTS STRESS ALCOHOLISM AS TRUE DISEASE

At the launching of *The Grapevine*, we wish to express our heartiest congratulations and best wishes for the success of this new publication. The invitation to contribute a note on the Yale Plan Clinics to the first issue of your Journal, confirms our belief in the close relation between the interests of Alcoholics Anonymous and the broad studies we have undertaken on all aspects of alcoholism.
The first Yale Plan Clinics, which are at New Haven and Hartford, were established by the Laboratory of Applied Physiology of ... University in cooperation with the Con... of the Clinics, the latter will limit their activity solely to the guiding of alcoholics to those facilities which according to diagnosis seem to be the most promising in the individual case. Such guidance is being practiced at present at the Clinics in bringing suitable cases into contact with the local groups of Alcoholics Anonymous. It goes without saying that one of our objectives is to further interest and confidence in Alcoholics Anonymous among those who have not heard of it or who are inadequately informed. The contacts of the Clinics with the courts, with various departments of State government and with civic agencies will contribute greatly to bring about adequate understanding of the nature of alcoholism, of the utilization of the existing, and the development of needed, facilities.
The Clinics in giving physical examinations ... come for advice bring... lishing clinics in other cities. The indications are that there is a wide interest in the rehabilitation of alcoholics and that only direction is needed to give it full display.
The problem of the alcoholic is too great to be solved by any one person or even by any one organization. The cooperation of all individuals and all organizations, based on mutual respect, and understanding of each other's aims, is needed to bring success to the efforts of all those who are interested in bringing back the alcoholic into the life of the community.

New Haven, Connecticut

Howard W. Haggard
E. M. Jellinek

"GRAPEVINE" IN BOW

In a big smoke-filled room six ink-stained ...wretches sipped at their Cokes as I shot ques...

EDITORIAL:

The Shape of Things to Come

In the book Alcoholics Anonymous there is a chapter called "A Vision for You". Wandering through it recently, my eye was caught by this startling paragraph written a short five years ago. *"Someday we hope that every alcoholic who journeys will find a Fellowship of Alcoholics Anonymous at his destination. To some extent this is already true. Some of us are salesmen and go about. Little clusters of twos and threes and fives of us have sprung up in other communities through contact with our two large centers----"* Rubbing my eyes I looked again. A lump came into my throat. "Only five years," I thought. "Then but two large centers—little clusters of twos and threes — travelers who hoped one day to find us at every destination."
Could it be that only yesterday this was just a hope—those little clusters of twos and threes, those little beacons so anxiously watched as they flickered, but never went out.
And today—hundreds of centers shedding their warm illumination upon the lives of thousands, lighting the dark shoals where the stranded and hopeless lie breaking up—those fingers of light already stretching to our beach heads in other lands.
Now comes another lighted lamp—this little newspaper called *"The Grapevine"*. May its rays of hope and ex-perience ever fall upon the current of our A.A. life and one day illumine every dark corner of this alcoholic world.
The aspirations of its editors, contributors and readers could well be voiced in the last words of *"A Vision for You"*. *"Abandon yourself to God as you understand God. Admit your faults to Him and your fellows. Clear away the wreckage of your past. Give freely of what you find, and join us. We shall be with you, in the Fellowship of The Spirit, and you will surely meet some of us as you trudge the Road of Happy Destiny. May God bless you and keep you—until then."*

Bill

wives are—they've got to feel they're the most influential factor in a husband's life. Point is, during all the years my wife tried to get me to quit I just got worse—then I catch up with A.A. and zingo—I get completely dried up and obviously like the procedure. So I'm afraid she feels there must be something lacking in my affection or why couldn't I have quit just for her?
It's obvious at the meetings that others in A.A. have been a lot smarter about this angle and maybe can help with a couple of suggestions. *Jim D.*

Dear Grapevine: I've been in A.A. a year and a month and I'm so happy, so glad at last, to be alive. A year and a month ago I wanted to die—although I didn't do anything about it except go on drinking, which is a pretty good way. My career, for I happen to be a writer, was at a standstill, and my way of living, my habits and emotions were as distorted as the view I used to see of myself in the bottom of a glass.
Now, very, very slowly, I am becoming the person I'm supposed to be. Normal habits and pleasures come back slowly. Things like enjoying food, gardening, going to the theatre, spending an evening with friends while conscious—all these habits had to be reformed, like a paralytic learning the re-use of his limbs. Just the other day I said to myself; "All right—you're fifteen years behind in your life. Fifteen years behind in your career. Thank God you came into A.A. when you did. Now you can begin, slowly, and get your life back." Perhaps some of you know this experience of discouraged impatience. Perhaps you've been sober a certain number of months and are beginning to say, "Well, so what?" Don't go out and get drunk, as I came so near doing a month ago. Weather this let-down period between first getting truly sober and getting yourself adjusted to life and living. Work like a beaver with an extra spurt of effort in, for and with A.A. That's the solution. I am sure of it. I had to write this because I'm so grateful again to A.A. for seeing me through these "growing pains". *Felicia G.*

Points of View:

The Grapevine welcomes letters from its reader-members. Please survey, however, the size of the sheet and keep your notes brief, because we'd like to print a fair cross-section, with as little cutting as possible.

Dear Grapevine: I was surely glad to learn that A.A. is planning to publish a "house-organ". I think a lot of newer members, like myself, who might incline to be shy about making personal contacts for help with their individual problems will welcome this means of communicating with experienced A.A.s. For example, I can hardly buttonhole a fellow-member at a meeting and bluntly say: "My wife is jealous of you!" Yet that's pretty much the situation which bothers me quite a lot. What I mean is that my Missus doesn't understand. She's delighted with the results of the past six months, but you know how

INTER GROUP MEETING IN MANHATTAN; Capitol Hotel, 51st Street and 8th Avenue, Walnut Room; every Tuesday evening at 8:30. Room open from 5:30. For all other meeting information watch group news on our Metropolitan Circuit page, and check each issue for changes of time and location.

ALCOHOLICS ANONYMOUS

Webster's definition—an act of giving time and power without stint, to helping others

Above is my version of the title "Alcoholics Anonymous" which you requested for publication. So far as using my name, I am very proud of the fact that I am a member of A.A. so you may use my name as the author of the enclosed if you wish. Wishing you all a lot of luck and a large circulation for *"The Grapevine"*. "Yours for Victory", Stewart A.S.

A. A. GOES TO SEA

Or rather the merchant seamen have discovered A.A.! Just over a year ago, Dr. Florence Powdermaker, a well-known psycho-analyst, sent us a patient—who promptly dried up, pleasing the good doctor no end. Then Dr. Powdermaker put on a Naval uniform and took up the problems of tired or shell-shocked seamen. Oddly enough she found that many of them had just the same problem we landlubbers are cursed with . . . they were alcoholics and they wanted the worst way to get over it. She tried the A.A. literature on them — the book and the pamphlets — and it worked!
When there got to be about 40 of them, those who were still ashore put their heads together. Like the rest of us, they wanted to help others recover—but they felt they had a special field in other seamen. They know seamen, and they know that most regular seamen look on landlubbers as almost a race apart. *Their* name for us is "shore people", and they don't easily feel at home with us. Add that to the alcoholic apartness—and you have something. So they figured they'd catch more seamen if they had their own group—for seamen only. But we're sure that will be only at the beginning—they'll find, as we did, that alcoholics are buddies under the skin, no matter what their profession or background, and as a matter of fact the original delegation who came to tell us of their plans and ask our co-operation, were instantly absorbed, to their own, and our, intense pleasure.
But if and when they form their own group and get their own clubhouse, we wish them all the luck in the world—as one drunk to another, fellows in A.A.

CORPORATION MEETS

The semi-annual corporation meeting was held at the 24th Street Club House on April 18th, 1944 at 8:00 P.M. Fifty-two members attended (A.A.s who have been dry a year or more).
The secretary read the minutes of the last meeting (September 29, 1943) and these were voted to be accepted, as read.
Due to illness of the president, the vice-president took the chair and suggested that we dispense with the current business, for the moment, in order to hear the new proposal of the Inter Group Committee. This was read and was followed by a discussion which brought to light the following facts: (1)—Only a minority of those present had foreknowledge of the proposed organizational change, (2)—the proposal was too lengthy and involved to be digested and voted on at the meeting, (3)—it was felt that it should be put up to the membership, at large, through the individual groups. It was, therefore, moved and voted that the following resolution be put into effect: "Resolved—that, though the corporation approves the basic ideas expressed in the plan submitted by the Inter Group Committee, it, the plan, or a condensation thereof, be submitted to the various groups for their approval. If and when this approval is forthcoming, it is suggested that each group select its two representatives to the new Central Committee and send their decision to the corporation secretary."
A motion was made to dissolve the corporation, but was withdrawn when it was pointed out that this could not be done without many legal complications taking several months.

A.A. in wartime
As World War II is fought overseas, the Fellowship does its part. An April 1943 article (right) in the Fort Worth, Texas, *Star-Telegram* reports that A.A. has reduced war-industries worker absenteeism due to alcoholism. The article states that the A.A. program has helped as many as 5,000 workers return to their jobs.

producer for such assistance. As speedily as other requests are received, national headquarters here plans to assign investigators from

the groups in the nearest localities to go to work on restoration of sick individuals to full efficiency in the same manner as thousands have been rebuilt in the eight years history of the movement.

remedy for excessive use of alcohol that will do the good that prohibition could not do because of obnoxious restriction of freedom. Two-thirds of the membership ac-

tive now have laid the foundation for permanent recovery while half the veterans, as they might be indexed, have had no relapse since joining the program, although they were often pronounced incurable.

> WINNING THE WAR WAS IMPORTANT TO JOE BUT WORK CAME SECOND TO 'BENDING AN ELBOW'

Box 459 opens to mail
"About Your Central Office," a bulletin distributed to A.A. groups by the Alcoholic Foundation, announces "As of May 1, 1944, our new address will be P.O. Box 459, Grand Central Station." Box 459 will become both the post office address and symbolic address of Alcoholics Anonymous, in its early days an organization that must rely heavily on mail.

Marty M. and the NCEA
Inspired largely by the efforts of Marty M., Dr. E.M. Jellinek, America's premier researcher in alcoholism, joins two other medical authorities to form the National Committee for Education on Alcohol (NCEA). On behalf of the NCEA, housed in a Yale University building (right), Marty embarks on a nationwide tour to tell of her struggle with alcoholism.

Women's prison groups begin to meet
The first women's prison group meets on March 18, 1944, at Clinton Farms in Clinton, New Jersey.

The first French-speaking group
Dave B. of Montreal, an ex-bank clerk and accountant who had slipped far down the ladder because of alcoholism, sobers up after reading the Big Book sent to him by his sister. He contacts A.A. in New York and soon starts holding meetings in his home, launching the first French-speaking A.A. group in the world. Some records cite the year of the first meeting as 1944, others as 1947.

1945 — 1954

First steps around the globe

London transport, 1952

After World War II ends, A.A. groups begin to spring up in other lands, with word of the fledgling organization spreading south of the border, across the Atlantic, and to the Pacific Rim. The decade also witnesses the Fellowship's first international convention and the creation of the General Service Conference.

Joining the fold...

Argentina	France	Nicaragua
Aruba	Germany	Norway
Australia	Guam	Okinawa
Bahamas	Iceland	Peru
Belgium	Ireland	Philippines
Bermuda	Jamaica	Puerto Rico
Brazil	Japan	Scotland
Chile	Korea	South Africa
Curaçao	Mexico	Sweden
Denmark	Morocco	Trinidad & Tobago
England	Netherlands	
Finland	New Zealand	Venezuela

A.A.'s tenth anniversary
More than 2,500 of the Fellowship's members and friends from 36 states and two Canadian provinces gather in Cleveland to honor Bill W. and Dr. Bob. Sponsored by the city's 44 groups, the two-day event includes open-house meetings, parties, a tea, an assembly at Severance Hall (below), and a closing dinner at the Carter Hotel. According to a Grapevine reporter, the speeches of Bill and Dr. Bob trace the development of A.A. with "gratitude, humility, and simplicity."

A magazine article's reach
"Maybe I Can Do It Too," an article about A.A. member Edward G. that ran in the October, 1944 edition of *Reader's Digest*, appears in translation in several of the magazine's international editions, as it will for the next four years. As a result, alcoholics from around the globe write to the Alcoholic Foundation seeking to learn more about the Fellowship.

1945–46

First meetings in Australia
In a letter to Archie McKinnon, a psychiatric nurse interested in helping alcoholics in Sydney, Bobbie B. of the Alcoholic Foundation provides the names of two other men who share the same aim: Dr. Sylvester Minogue and Fr. Tom Dunlea, the founder of Boystown in Australia. The three nonalcoholics band together to form the country's first A.A. group, with Rex A. the first member to achieve and maintain sobriety.

African-American groups spring up
Early in 1945, five African-American residents of St. Louis form a group that quickly expands. In Washington D.C., Jim S., sponsored by a local A.A. named Charlie, begins to hold meetings in a rented room at a local YMCA; Jim later helps start the first group in Harlem. By 1950, African-Americans will have formed groups in Detroit, Chicago, Philadelphia, Los Angeles, Cleveland, and other cities and towns. In a country of great diversity, A.A. groups will welcome all races.

An Atlantic outpost
After seeking advice from the Alcoholic Foundation, Steve V., an A.A. member formerly of Trenton, N.J., forms a group in St. Georges, Bermuda. It jumps from two to six members within a month and grows quickly thereafter. The next year, the *Hamilton Mid-Ocean News* will publish a series of twelve articles on Alcoholics Anonymous.

The lighter side

The reports and letters printed in the Grapevine are leavened with the occasional alcohol-related cartoon, like the "Down Alibi Alley" submission by a member (below). Early editions of the magazine also include a jokes column called "Barley CORN!!"

DOWN ALIBI ALLEY: with Hal H. of Chicago . . . .

Trustees issue statement on fund-raising

In an effort to halt attempts by various charities to ride the coattails of A.A.'s ascendancy, the Alcoholic Foundation issues a statement aimed at organizations that imply sponsorship by A.A. in their personal appeals to the public. It reads, in part,

"Alcoholics Anonymous not only fails to endorse the present solicitation of funds but looks with disfavor on the unauthorized use of its name in any fund-raising activity."

Overtures from Hollywood

In the wake of the success of *The Lost Weekend*—the Oscar-winning 1945 film about a struggling alcoholic—three Hollywood studios offer A.A. as much as $100,000 for rights to the Fellowship's story. The Alcoholic Foundation, fearing such films would amount to a violation of privacy, refuses the offers on behalf of A.A. members.

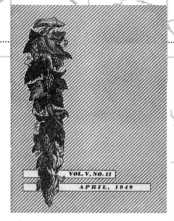

Ireland joins the program

The decision of a Philadelphia A.A. member and former tavern owner, Connor F., to travel to Ireland leads to the formation of the first Irish group. Connor and his wife visit a Dublin sanitarium, where a doctor introduces them to patient Richard P. of Belfast. After reading the Big Book presented to him by Connor, Richard writes to a number of contacts who had learned of A.A. through Fr. Tom Dunlea. (Dunlea, a nonalcoholic and one of the founders of Australia's first group, had spread the message on a trip home to Ireland.) Before long, Ireland's inaugural A.A. group is meeting in a room at the Country Shop on Dublin's St. Stephen's Green.

The Twelve Traditions published

One by one, the Twelve Traditions developed by Bill W. are put into print for the first time. The medium is The Grapevine, now in a compact booklet format.

VOL. V, NO. 11
APRIL, 1949

First meetings in Mexico

Americans Lester F. and Pauline D. organize a group for Mexico City's English-speaking community. Meanwhile, a Mexican resident of Cleveland, Ricardo P., translates portions of the Big Book into Spanish. The importation of Spanish-language alcoholism-related publications and the creation of Spanish-speaking A.A. groups is approved at a late-summer conference of Mexico's Board of Public Information.

National Palace, Mexico City

A meeting place, Dublin

A.A. in the news

The rapid growth of A.A. is reflected in the increasing press coverage the society receives. The Kings Feature Syndicate article shown at right appeared in newspapers nationwide in the spring of 1946. It focused on women alcoholics, whose A.A. membership was growing in leaps and bounds.

Inroads into Africa

In 1946, the A.A. movement springs to life in South Africa in three different places. The founders, unknown to one another, are Arthur S., who reads of A.A. in *Reader's Digest*, contacts the Alcoholic Foundation and, with social workers, two ministers, and a psychiatrist, forms a group in Johannesburg; Pat O'G., of Capetown, who also has consulted the Alcoholic Foundation; and Val D., who achieves sobriety after reading a copy of the Big Book handed to him by a priest and soon starts a group in the town of Springs.

First stirrings in England

Though the first official A.A. group in England won't be formed until 1948, the ball gets rolling when a visiting American woman, Grace O., writes to five Londoners who are in touch with the Alcoholic Foundation and schedules a meeting at the Dorchester Hotel (right) for March 31, 1947. The eight attendees include two A.A. members from North America: an A.A. from Hollywood, California, whose acquaintance she had made on the voyage across the Atlantic, and "Canadian Bob," whom Grace had met in a London restaurant and who will figure large in A.A.'s growth. Meetings will continue in restaurants and residences, among them the home of Canadian Bob.

A Swedish "offshoot"

Frank B., a Swedish-American who had become sober in Newark, New Jersey, moves to Sweden and reports to the Newark group that he has joined an A.A. group in the town of Borås—much to the surprise of the Alcoholic Foundation. The group is in fact affiliated with the Links Society. (Founded by an officer of the Temperance Board in Stockholm, the Links Society was loosely based on the A.A. concepts, with which the officer had become familiar on a trip to the U.S. in 1939.) An exchange of letters between the Foundation and the secretary of the Borås Links group ensues, leading to a listing with A.A. in February 1948. In later years, more Swedish groups will shift their affiliation from the Links Society to A.A. and the Swedish G.S.O. will issue the Twelve Steps in booklet form (above).

1947—48

Servicemen launch groups in the Pacific

In the wake of World War II, American servicemen stationed at military bases in the Pacific launch A.A. groups, with the Alcoholic Foundation acting as facilitator. In the summer of 1947, a group in Guam grows from four members to 24 in one month. In Okinawa, the Pioneer Group begins meeting in the fall of 1947.

A.A. becomes self-supporting

Bill W. reports that income from the Big Book and contributions from individual A.A. groups have made the Alcoholic Foundation self-supporting. The idea of donations grew from an estimate that all expenses could be met if each group were to send the Foundation a sum equal to $1 per member per year. Donations were entirely voluntary, and equal service was provided to all groups regardless of their contribution record—a policy still in effect today.

A mission to Norway

George F., a Norwegian immigrant and coffee shop owner in Connecticut, writes home after many years to share the good news of his sobriety through A.A. When he learns that his brother, a typesetter for an Oslo newspaper, is an alcoholic one step from ruin, George and his wife sell their shop and move to Norway. After initially showing no interest in the Twelve Steps, George's brother takes the message to heart and becomes sober almost immediately. Placing small ads in his paper, he eventually recruits enough alcoholics to form Norway's first group.

Oslo Harbor

The A.A. preamble

In the June, 1947 edition of the Grapevine, a preamble defining the Fellowship and its mission appears for the first time. The Preamble is quickly adopted by A.A. groups and becomes a standard inclusion in A.A. literature.

A fitful start in Brazil

After two years of sporadic correspondence between the Alcoholic Foundation and a few American residents of Brazil, the Foundation registers Herb D. as an A.A. official contact. In September 1947, Herb requests and receives a batch of A.A. pamphlets and the name of another A.A. member living in Rio de Janeiro. The two men seek members and the first group in Brazil takes shape.

Sugarloaf Mountain, Rio de Janeiro

Expansion in Canada

By late 1947, Alcoholics Anonymous groups begin to form in the Maritime Provinces of Nova Scotia, New Brunswick, Prince Edward Island, and Newfoundland. The Fellowship is now country-wide, with groups having been founded in Ontario in 1943, Quebec in 1944, Alberta and Manitoba in 1945, British Columbia in 1946, and Saskatchewan in 1947.

A meeting place in Cheticamp, Nova Scotia

Finland gets the message

A few alcoholics join weekly meetings at the home of a couple employed by the Helsinki Welfare Office. Along with "Mom and Dad," as the leaders are called, they learn of Alcoholics Anonymous when "Maybe I Can Do It Too" appears in the Finnish edition of *Reader's Digest*.

The group soon begins to adhere to the principles of both A.A. and the Sweden-born Links Society. In years hence, Finnish groups will become connected to A.A. The placard at right reads "First Things First."

Start-ups in Korea

In early 1948, a nonalcoholic priest named Father Mosley starts a group in Seoul after he receives A.A. literature from New York. Two other groups meet sporadically over the next three years, but the first group to be listed with the Alcoholic Foundation will not be formed until 1952: Yong Dong Po, named after the town in which it first meets.

Akron marks its thirteenth anniversary

Some 4,000 A.A. members from Ohio gather in Akron to celebrate another milestone. The meeting, attended by both Bill W. and Dr. Bob, opens with a prayer from Rev. Walter F. Tunks, the Episcopal rector who had referred Bill to Henrietta Seiberling in 1935.

New Zealand's first group

Ian McE., a resident of the South Island town of Richmond, voluntarily submits himself to a psychiatric hospital in an effort to sober up. There, he comes across the *Reader's Digest* article "Maybe I Can Do It Too". Struck by his identification with the article's subject, he writes to Bobbie B. of the Alcoholic Foundation. His letter launches a long-term correspondence with (and sponsorship by) Bobbie that will lead to the formation of the first New Zealand group.

Movement in the Philippines

Mildred G., a globe-trotting A.A. member, serves as the Alcoholic Foundation's contact after she and her husband arrive in Manila in August, 1950. She later reports her intention to start a group. Exactly when the first group is formed is unclear, but by 1955 Filipinos and expatriates are meeting in 11 groups throughout the country.

....1949–51

A.A.'s post-war boom in Japan

After an article on A.A. appears in *Pacific Stars and Stripes*, the Alcoholic Foundation is flooded with letters from American servicemen based in Japan. The Foundation forwards their names to Harry G., who was in Tokyo writing a book on the War Crime Trials of 1945–48. (Harry had written the Foundation in December 1947, suggesting that Japan was fertile ground for A.A.) He and an A.A. member from Indiana start an English-speaking group, leading to the establishment of native groups across Japan.

Pagoda in Japan

Dr. Bob's illness

In the summer of 1948, Dr. Bob learns he has terminal cancer, leading him to shut down his office and retire from medical practice.

The Scottish messenger

In 1948, Sir Philip D., a Scottish gentleman farmer who has long struggled with alcoholism, travels to the U.S. at the invitation of the Oxford Group. There he meets A.A. member George R., who acquaints him with the Fellowship's principles. Sir Philip returns home determined to stop drinking and to carry the A.A. message. He succeeds, and Scotland's first groups are founded in May 1949 in Edinburgh and Glasgow, where meetings are held in the St. Enoch Hotel (right).

Rapid growth in Holland

In January 1949, Henk Krauweel, of the Medical Bureau for Alcohol in Amsterdam, reports to the Alcoholic Foundation that he and two of his patients, John V. and Carel A., intend to organize an A.A. meeting in mid-February. They do so, and with much success. In the next two years, a number of groups will be started in Rotterdam, Haarlem, The Hague, and other Dutch cities.

An Amsterdam canal

A.A.'s first international convention

In July 1950, Alcoholics Anonymous's 15th anniversary is marked with an international convention in Cleveland, with some 3,000 people in attendance. One of the most significant events is the adoption of the Twelve Traditions. The convention, held at the Cleveland Public Auditorium (above), also features the last message to the Fellowship by Dr. Bob, who stresses kindness and "keeping it simple."

INTERIOR OF THE CLEVELAND PUBLIC AUDITORIUM, CLEVELAND, OHIO   9

CLEVELAND PUBLIC AUDITORIUM • JULY 28 to 30. 1950

Bill W. addresses the American Psychiatric Association

At the invitation of Dr. Kirby Collier of Rochester, New York, one of A.A.'s earliest admirers in the psychiatric profession, Bill W. participates in an alcoholism symposium at the American Psychiatric Association convention in Montreal. His address marks the acceptance of A.A. by yet another major American medical organization.

Denmark: From Ring i Ring to A.A.

In 1950, a group belonging to a national temperance society called Ring i Ring, founded in 1948 by Dr. Martinson, inventor of the drug Antabuse, is visited by American A.A. member Gordon McD. and his wife. It meets in a restaurant (right) at Copenhagen's zoo. Soon after, the group changes its name to "Ring i Ring, Danish A.A." and registers with the Alcoholic Foundation. In the next few years, other Ring i Ring members will break away and hold closed meetings based on the Twelve Steps and other A.A. principles.

The arrival of Al-Anon

In loosely organized Family Groups, loved ones of A.A. members had shared their experiences since the Fellowship's earliest days. At Bill W.'s urging, his wife Lois moves to create a separate fellowship that will formalize these meetings. With Anne B., who had initiated a Family Group in Westchester County, New York, Lois sends a letter to 87 such groups suggesting that they unite under the name of Al-Anon. The response is positive, and in January 1952 Lois and Anne will shift the growing organization's office from Stepping Stones to the 24th Street Clubhouse in Manhattan.

A.A.'s first General Service Conference

The first General Service Conference, orchestrated by chairman of the Alcoholic Foundation Bernard Smith, is held in April 1951 at the Commodore Hotel in New York. Bill W. later writes of its momentousness: "The delegates . . . listened to reports from the Board of Trustees and from all of the services. There was warm but cordial debate on many questions of A.A. policy… [It was proved] as never before that A.A.'s Tradition Two was correct: Our group conscience could safely act as the sole authority and sure guide for Alcoholics Anonymous."

A prestigious award

In San Francisco on October 30, 1951, the American Public Health Association presents Alcoholics Anonymous with the Lasker Award, "in recognition of its unique and highly successful approach" to an "age-old public health and social problem." The award is made possible through benefactions of Mary and Albert Lasker, New York philanthropists. A ceremony on the previous evening, with Bill W. and Board of Trustees chairman Bernard Smith as speakers, is attended by some 3,000 A.A.s and family members, physicians, public health experts, and clergymen. In the newspaper photograph above, Smith is shown at far left.

Peru's inaugural group

After reading in *Look* magazine about ACE, a treatment for acute alcoholism, Percy N., an American living in Lima, writes to the Alcoholic Foundation asking for its view of the treatment. The Foundation responds by sending him three Alcoholics Anonymous pamphlets. In turn, Percy expresses his wish to become a member and start a group, which he proceeds to do in November 1950. While his initial translations of literature give the impression of a "cure" and stress religion, an A.A. member visiting Lima explains to him the true principles of the program, putting Percy's group and those that follow on the right track.

Plaza des Armas, Lima

The death of Dr. Bob

Dr. Bob dies of cancer on November 15, 1950. During the Akron physician's 15 years of sobriety, the Fellowship he started with Bill W. had transformed the lives of close to 100,000 men and women and their loved ones.

Caribbean by way of Canada

Burton L., an A.A. member from Toronto now living in Nassau, forms the first group in the Bahamas—four members who meet on Sunday afternoons. The group, one of the first in the Caribbean, makes a contribution of $6 when it registers with the Alcoholic Foundation.

A post-war beginning in Germany

A handful of U.S. servicemen, all recovering alcoholics stationed at U.S. Army Base I Munich after the end of World War II, take on the responsibility of forming the first A.A. group in Germany. On a mission to sober up local alcoholics, they post notices of a meeting to be held at Hotel Leopold (right) on November 1, 1953. Among the 25 attendees are Max, Kurt, and Heindrich, who will meet with the Americans in what will come to be called Germany's "mother group."

1952–54

A.A. in Argentina

In the early 1950s, Hector G. of Buenos Aires is rescued from alcoholism after reading *Alcoholics Anonymous* and seeking the aid of a physician. He writes to the Alcoholic Foundation, which sends him A.A. literature in Spanish and asks permission to list him as a contact for referrals. Hector founds Argentina's first group, and in 1955 will report that its members are relishing their newfound sobriety.

Buenos Aires skyline

Twelve Steps and Twelve Traditions is published

Bill W. becomes increasingly devoted to writing projects, one of which emerges as *Twelve Steps and Twelve Traditions*—the book that sets forth his deepest understanding of A.A.'s basic principles.

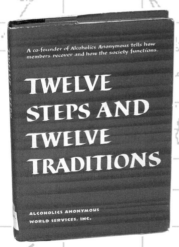

Nicaragua's inaugural group

In the fall of 1953, Grupo de A.A. La Merced is founded in León by Jack M., who took up residence in Nicaragua in 1950 and joined A.A. when he briefly returned to the United States for cancer treatment. Groups in the capital city of Managua and other Nicaraguan population centers will start meeting a decade later, facilitated by the Alcoholic Foundation.

The Big Book hits Belgium

At a gathering of English-speaking and Belgian alcoholics in Brussels, Jean L. introduces the Big Book and the principles of Alcoholics Anonymous. Within

Grand Place, Brussels

months of the October, 1953 meeting, groups start assembling not only in Belgium's capital but also in cities and towns in Flanders and Wallonia.

Bill W. declines honorary degrees

In the wake of Alcoholic Anonymous's success, several colleges and universities offer Bill W. honorary degrees. He declines, explaining why in this excerpt from a letter to Yale University, which had proposed an honorary Doctor of Laws degree:

> "The tradition of Alcoholics Anonymous …entreats each member to avoid all that particular kind of personal publicity or distinction which might link his name with our Society in the general public mind."

He then quotes A.A.'s need for anonymity, as stated in Tradition Twelve.

The Alcoholic Foundation becomes the General Service Board

Changing the name of the Alcoholic Foundation to the General Service Board of Alcoholics Anonymous was first proposed at the first General Service Conference in the spring of 1951, but the switch becomes official only in 1954. The motivation is to signal that the A.A. membership is taking full responsibility for itself.

Membership exceeds 100,000

By the end of A.A.'s second decade, some

130,000 members

are meeting in approximately

6,000 groups on five continents.

1955 — 1964

A.A. comes of age

The St. Louis Convention of 1955 affirms the Fellowship's maturity as Bill W. passes to the members the responsibility for A.A.'s Three Legacies of recovery, unity, and service. The convention signals a decade of change— one that sees the consolidation of family groups under the name of Al-Anon, a separate fellowship that, like Alcoholics Anonymous, has spread to almost every corner of the world.

Joining the fold...

Austria	Fiji	Portugal
Barbados	Greece	Singapore
British	Grenada	Southern
Honduras	Guatemala	Rhodesia
(Belize)	Honduras	(Zimbabwe)
Ceylon	India	Spain
(Sri Lanka)	Jordan	Switzerland
Colombia	Northern	Taiwan
Costa Rica	Rhodesia	Tanzania
Dominican	(Zambia)	Turkey
Republic	Papua-New	Wales
El Salvador	Guinea	

Guatemalan coffee plantation, c. 1955

Mr. Eddie of El Salvador

Edward F., who has carried the Fellowship's message to several alcoholics in Boston and San Francisco, moves to San Salvador with his Salvadoran wife. After find-

Current G.S.O., San Salvador

ing it hard to arouse interest in A.A., a friend of his wife introduces Edward to her alcoholic uncle, Don A., and the two men form a group that meets at the home of Atilio, a wealthy alcoholic. As membership grows, meetings are moved to the Garcia Flamenco school building. "Mr. Eddie," as he becomes known, will later help start groups in other Central American countries.

First meetings in Madrid

A Mrs. Garcia of New York informs G.S.O. New York of the wish of Dr. E. Pelaz, a psychiatrist at a Madrid sanitarium, to launch an A.A. group. G.S.O. New York sends Pelaz pamphlets and the name of its Madrid contact, American expatriate Ray C. Ray and fellow alcoholic Dan C. begin holding English-language meetings in June 1955. By the end of the year membership has increased fourfold and a Spanish-American group is meeting at Pelaz's sanitarium. Before long, the Spaniards form a separate group, which quickly attracts more members and spurs the formation of A.A. groups countrywide.

1955

A historic International Convention

Some 5,000 people attend the second International Convention in St. Louis (right). Among the important events at this 20th anniversary gathering is Bill's presentation on A.A. history and the importance of understanding it. In addition, the second edition of the Big Book is launched, and Al-Anon, now four years old, participates in five workshops. President Dwight D. Eisenhower recognizes the occasion with a congratulatory telegram (right).

Second Edition of Big Book published

The second edition of *Alcoholics Anonymous* reflects the membership's growing diversity. The chapters on A.A. principles remain the same, and eight of the stories of early members' efforts to achieve sobriety are retained in a section called "Pioneers of A.A." In addition, 24 new stories appear in two separate sections: "They Stopped in Time" and "They Lost Nearly All." The Twelve Traditions are added as well.

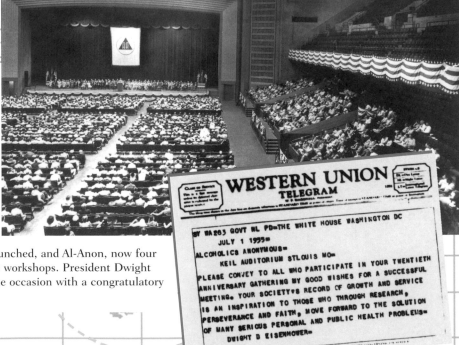

WESTERN UNION
TELEGRAM

BY WA 263 GOVT NL PD=THE WHITE HOUSE WASHINGTON DC
JULY 1 1955=
ALCOHOLICS ANONYMOUS=
KEIL AUDITORIUM STLOUIS MO=
PLEASE CONVEY TO ALL WHO PARTICIPATE IN YOUR TWENTIETH
ANNIVERSARY GATHERING MY GOOD WISHES FOR A SUCCESSFUL
MEETING. YOUR SOCIETYS RECORD OF GROWTH AND SERVICE
IS AN INSPIRATION TO THOSE WHO THROUGH RESEARCH,
PERSEVERANCE AND FAITH, MOVE FORWARD TO THE SOLUTION
OF MANY SERIOUS PERSONAL AND PUBLIC HEALTH PROBLEMS=
DWIGHT D EISENHOWER=

Bill W. passes the torch

The St. Louis convention culminates with Bill officially handing leadership of A.A. over to the members. The resolution he reads is passed with a roar of approval:

"Be it therefore resolved that the General Service Conference… should become as of this date… the guardian of the Traditions of Alcoholics Anonymous, the perpetuators of the world services of our Society, the voice of the group conscience of our entire Fellowship, and the sole successors of its co-founders, Doctor Bob and Bill."

Venezuela joins the fold

A few Americans who gather for A.A. meetings in Caracas place a small ad in a local English-language newspaper. It draws the attention of Christiaan V., who has previously sought to start a Spanish-speaking group. With the help of the Americans, Christiaan carries the message to Luis and Clyde, and the three men become the first link in a chain of groups that will spread across Venezuela.

A bulletin for Loners

Hundreds of Loners—individuals who are listed with A.A. but do not belong to a group— are being mailed G.S.O.'s monthly bulletin: *A.A. Loners Meeting,* each issue of which features personal stories of Loners from around the world. The stated purpose is to enable such members "to share A.A. love and gratitude, strength and faith with one another." A previous bulletin—*The Internationalists Round Robin,* in 1949—had grown out of the efforts of Captain Jack S., a sailor who found sobriety in A.A. and maintained it by exchanging letters with groups he helped start around the world.

1956–58

The Third Legacy

At the St. Louis Convention, Bill speaks of the Fellowship's Third Legacy, that of Service. In his words, ". . . an A.A. service is anything whatever that helps us to reach a fellow sufferer. . .from the Twelfth Step itself to a ten-cent phone call and a cup of coffee, and to A.A.'s General Service Office for national and international action." Fifty thousand Third Legacy booklets (above right), known today as the A.A. Service Manual, will be printed and distributed to A.A. groups.

A.A. COMES OF AGE   JULY 1-2-3, 1955
20th ANNIVERSARY CONVENTION, ST. LOUIS, MO.

The
THIRD LEGACY MANUAL
Of World Service
As Proposed By
BILL.

A.A.'s first overseas General Service Board

The quick growth of Alcoholics Anonymous in Great Britain and Ireland makes apparent the need for a separate General Service Board. After seeking guidance from G.S.O. New York, representatives from England, Wales, Scotland and Ireland meet in London on October 28, 1956. They resolve to establish a Board of Trustees based on the U.S. model, to be known as the General Service Board of Alcoholics Anonymous in Great Britain & Ireland, Ltd. The first G.S.B. outside the U.S., housed in London's Fruit Exchange (right), will begin operations in 1957.

North American hospital groups

By the beginning of 1957, the General Service Office in New York is maintaining contact with 230 hospital groups in the United States and Canada—the legacy of the pioneering A.A. groups formed two decades earlier at St. Thomas Hospital in Akron and Towns and Knickbocker hospitals in New York.

Letters from Greece

An American pilot who is an A.A. member reports to G.S.O. New York that he has presented a copy of *Twelve Steps and Twelve Traditions* to Rev. Charles Hanna, pastor of the American Church in Athens. Rev. Hanna begins corresponding with G.S.O. New York in early 1957. His efforts bring together three American Loners living in Athens—Frank O. and servicemen Gus and Cal—who hold Greece's first A.A. meeting in Athen's port city of Piraeus.

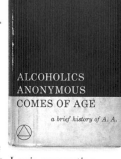

India: Loners no more

In January 1957, Charley M., an A.A. member employed by the National Film Board of Canada, contacts Sylvia M. and Supatti M., both New Delhi Loners listed with G.S.O. New York. (Charley had expressed to the office his wish to stay active in A.A. during a 36-month business sojourn in Asia.) The three place an ad in local newspapers, drawing responses from seven alcoholics—among them Mahindar S. G., who, like Sylvia and Supatti, is already listed. By May, New Delhi meetings are attracting eight to 12 people; by year's end, groups will be active in Calcutta and Bombay. Shown at right is a greeting card sent by a Bombay group to Bill and Lois in December 1961.

Best Wishes

To
Dear Bill and Lois
With love and gratitude.

A hearty Christmas greeting
That is meant to bring
your way
The very best of wishes
For a merry Christmas Day
And wishes for the new year—
May it truly be for you
A year of luck and real
success
In everything you do.

From
Stan G, Harold M, Louis P,
and all others of "AA"
XMAS·1961   India   Bombay.

A landmark book

In *Alcoholics Anonymous Comes of Age*, published October 1, 1957, Bill recounts A.A. history from a personal standpoint and then reviews the proceedings of the St. Louis convention. A section describing the Three Legacies is included, as are talks by A.A. friends in the fields of religion and medicine.

ALCOHOLICS ANONYMOUS COMES OF AGE
a brief history of A. A.

First International Conference of Young People in A.A.

In late April 1958, the first conference for A.A.'s younger members (then defined as those under age 40) is held at Hotel Niagara in Niagara Falls, New York. The *A.A. Exchange Bulletin* (the precursor to *Box 4-5-9*) reports that the purpose of the International Conference of Young People in A.A. (ICYPAA) is "to provide delegates with a thorough rundown of the application of our A.A. program to the individual difficulties encountered by young people in dealing not only with alcoholism but also with the other problems peculiar to their generation." ICYPAA is held annually.

Niagara Falls

The arrival of Alateen

Concern for the problems of the children of alcoholics, the topic of a special session at the 1955 St. Louis Convention, increases as letters from teenagers (a few of whom had started groups of their peers) begin to flow into the Al-Anon office. As a result, Al-Anon founds Alateen in 1957 and publishes the booklet *Youth and the Alcoholic Parent* (above).

YOUTH
AND THE ALCOHOLIC PARENT

A E C G

A MESSAGE TO YOUNG PEOPLE

Signing on in Singapore

Dick D., who regularly corresponds with G.S.O. New York, writes in March 1958 that the Singapore group now has 12 members and two likely prospects. (The group had begun meeting the previous year). One of the highlights of a recent gathering, Dick reports, was a visit from Charley M., the Canadian who had been instrumental in starting A.A. groups in India.

Singapore skyline

Dramatizations of alcoholism

When called upon, Alcoholics Anonymous plays an advisory role in the dramatization of alcoholism on television or in movies. In one instance, G.S.O. New York staff members work closely with scriptwriter J. P. Miller in preparation for the October 1958 broadcast of *The Days of Wine and Roses*, a "Playhouse 90" production. The play, examining the lives of an alcoholic married couple seeking help from A.A., will reach an international audience when it is produced as a movie in 1962; a poster for the film is shown below.

JACK LEMMON and LEE REMICK in DAYS OF WINE AND ROSES

State of the Structure

As a service to readers, the March 1958 Grapevine prints a chart outlining A.A.'s services and the Conference structure. Text in the top box notes that "over 7,000 groups, including 500 in hospitals, prisons, and other institutions and 760 overseas, are registered at the General Service Headquarters."

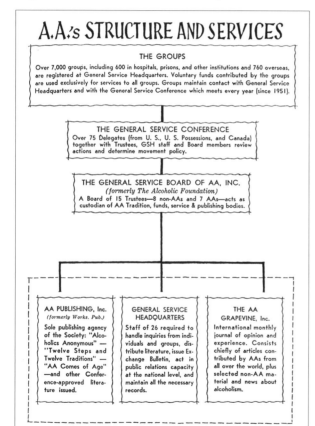

A.A.'s STRUCTURE AND SERVICES

THE GROUPS

Over 7,000 groups, including 600 in hospitals, prisons, and other institutions and 760 overseas, are registered at General Service Headquarters. Voluntary funds contributed by the groups are used exclusively for services to all groups. Groups maintain contact with General Service Headquarters and with the General Service Conference which meets every year (since 1951).

THE GENERAL SERVICE CONFERENCE

Over 75 Delegates (from U. S., U. S. Possessions, and Canada) together with Trustees, GSH staff and Board members review actions and determine movement policy.

THE GENERAL SERVICE BOARD OF AA, INC.

(formerly The Alcoholic Foundation)

A Board of 15 Trustees—8 non-AAs and 7 AAs—acts as custodian of AA Tradition, funds, service & publishing bodies.

AA PUBLISHING, Inc. *(formerly Works. Pub.)*	GENERAL SERVICE HEADQUARTERS	THE AA GRAPEVINE, Inc.
Sole publishing agency of the Society: "Alcoholics Anonymous" — "Twelve Steps and Twelve Traditions" — "AA Comes of Age" —and other Conference-approved literature issued.	Staff of 26 required to handle inquiries from individuals and groups, distribute literature, issue Exchange Bulletin, act in public relations capacity at the national level, and maintain all the necessary records.	International monthly journal of opinion and experience. Consists chiefly of articles contributed by AAs from all over the world, plus selected non-AA material and news about alcoholism.

Austria West, Austria East

In 1959, two A.A. members from Reichenall, Germany, decide to carry the message across the Austrian border to Salzburg. With the aid of their first contact, a physician from a local clinic for nervous diseases, they help a few alcoholics form a group. To the east in Vienna, two alcoholic women who are being treated in the clinic of a psychiatrist, Dr. Rotter, hear of A.A. and found a group on their own. With a gentleman from Linz, they begin to hold meetings in private homes. Both groups independently seek the advice of German groups and receive German-language A.A. literature. A current Vienna meeting place is shown at right.

1959—60

Colombia: Seven years to success

After years of failed attempts, a stable Colombian A.A. group is finally formed in January 1959. The principal players are Arturo E. of Medellín and Alejandro S. of Baranquilla, who had met while being treated for alcoholism in a Baranquilla clinic in 1952. While the men twice tried to launch a group (Alejandro, a prosperous businessman, had become familiar with A.A. principles while undergoing treatment in a Miami hospital), only Arturo is able to stay sober and carry through. His first group, which meets in Medellín, plants the seed for those that will follow in Bogotá and other Colombian cities.

France's first French-speaking groups

While American A.A.s had met in Paris as early as 1949, the first French-speaking group forms after the newspaper *France Soir* runs a series of articles on Alcoholics Anonymous by journalist Joseph Kessel in the summer of 1960. A letter to the journal from Manuel M. (originally from Spain) results in his receipt of A.A. literature and the start of a group of four—Manuel, François B., Jean M., and Lennard (a Swede). In 1961 the group, which takes the name Groupe Quai d'Orsay, will gain the sponsorship of expatriate Americans who established an A.A. group in Paris in 1955. More groups are formed, growth accelerates, and in the early 1970s France's General Service Office will open in Rue Trousseau (above).

Guatemala gets going

Guatemala's first A.A. group begins meeting in January 1960, through the efforts of Miguel Angel R. and Paulino G. The seed had been planted four years before by Reinaldo G., a friend of Miguel's who had joined A.A. in San Francisco before returning home to Guatemala. An Intergroup Service Office will open three years later. The flyer shown above announces a public meeting to be held in May 1967.

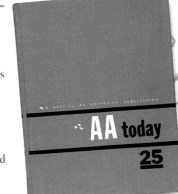

The third International Convention

Long Beach, California, plays host to A.A.'s 25th Anniversary celebration in July 1960. Some 8,900 attendees are joined by many of the Fellowship's historic figures—among them Bill and Lois, Sister Ignatia, Marty M., Dr. Jack Norris, Warden Clinton Duffy, and Dr. Harry Tiebout, a psychiatrist who championed A.A. and brought Marty M. into the program.

AA Today published

The Grapevine commemorates the 25th anniversary of Alcoholics Anonymous with the publication of the book *AA Today,* which features essays by Aldous Huxley, Reinhold Niebuhr, Dr. E. M. Jellinek, and other distinguished supporters.

Costa Rica's struggling start

Although the Costa Rican government's Committee on Alcoholism (COA), established in 1954, had some success in treating alcoholics, the only connection to A.A. was a perfunctory reading of the Twelve Steps at meetings. After a shaky beginning in 1958, A.A. Grupo Tradicionalista No.1—started by a small group of COA patients—becomes stable in 1959. By the summer of 1963, eight groups will be meeting countrywide and a General Service Office will open in San José.

An influential best seller

Avec les Alcooliques Anonymes ("With Alcoholics Anonymous"), a book by French journalist Joseph Kessel published in 1961, spurs the growth of A.A. in France and Germany. It depicts Alcoholics Anonymous as Kessel observed the organization during an extended stay in New York. A translation is published in Great Britain in the same year with the title *The Enemy in the Mouth*. In 1962, an American publisher releases the book as *The Road Back: A Report on Alcoholics Anonymous.*

THE ROAD BACK

A Report on Alcoholics Anonymous by JOSEPH KESSEL

The brilliant French journalist, author of THE LION, takes us on an exploratory voyage into the nightmare world of alcoholism

St. George's harbor, Grenada

Island hopping in the Caribbean

A.A. groups in the Caribbean, including those in the Bahamas (first group established in 1951) and Trinidad (1956), receive support in 1962 when the dedicated Gordon MacD. visits the Antilles and meets with secretaries of the groups in the region. The aim of what is called "the Caribbean Crusade," launched by Gordon and other members in 1959, is to develop and reinforce A.A. in the Caribbean and to facilitate cooperation between Caribbean and Latin American groups. Among the islands joining the fold in 1962 are Barbados and Grenada, both in the Lesser Antilles.

19**61–62**

Bill writes to Carl Jung

In a letter to Dr. Carl Jung, the Swiss-German psychoanalyst, Bill expresses his gratitude for Jung's long-ago message to Rowland G., who was treated by Jung and who would later lead friend Ebby T. to the Oxford Group. Bill wrote,

"You frankly told [Rowland] of the hopelessness of…further medical or psychiatric treatment," [and also of the possibility of] "a spiritual awakening or religious experience—in short, a genuine conversion."

Bill described these statements as "beyond doubt the first foundation stone upon which [A.A.] has been built." Jung responds with a gracious letter (right) confirming that the most appropriate antidote to alcoholism is spirituality, which is emphasized in the Twelve Steps.

Big Book sales top half a million

By 1961, more than 500,000 copies of *Alcoholics Anonymous* have been sold, including editions translated into Spanish, French, and German.

Dr. Norris elected Chairman

Dr. John L. Norris, the medical director of Eastman Kodak and a nonalcoholic trustee of A.A. since 1948, becomes chairman of the General Service Board. "Dr. Jack," described by Bill as "a most selfless and devoted worker," will be instrumental in the development of Regional Forums. His involvement with A.A. will continue after he steps down from the Board of Trustees in 1975.

Seamen meet in Houston

Internationalists sometimes grab the chance to meet, and in 1961 seaman Red R., spending a month in Texas, reports a gathering to *A.A. Exchange Bulletin:* "On May 22 we held a seamen's meeting in Houston at the 24 Hour Club. We had seven seamen, all sober and doing fine....The welcome mat is out for all seafarers in this area and we hope the group will grow...."

Following in A.A.'s footsteps

The Alcoholics Anonymous model for recovery is adopted by a number of emerging support groups. A news article in the December 29, 1961 edition of the *Wall Street Journal* notes the founding of Narcotics Anonymous, Gamblers Anonymous, and other fellowships based on mutual support and anonymity.

Introducing Victor E.

Victor E., the creation of a Grapevine editor, makes his first appearance in the magazine's July 1962 edition. In the cartoon shown below and all that follow, fate in one form or another—a passerby, a falling flowerpot, a black cat—intervenes to help Victor resist entering a saloon.

Victor E.

UK island groups

Guernsey gets on board in 1961 when Pru, a Loner, arranges for meetings to be held in the study of the headmaster of St. Joseph's Roman Catholic School in St. Peter Port. When the group moves to a room above a café, membership grows from six to a dozen. But not until the group finds a permanent home at Princess Elizabeth Hospital in 1981 will it undergo significant growth. A group starts meeting in the nearby island of Jersey in 1962, and small inter-island conventions are held for four or five years—in Guernsey in autumn, in Jersey in spring. The first A.A. group on the Isle of Mann, to the north in the Irish Sea, will be formed in 1966.

Two starts in the Dominican Republic

Two A.A. groups begin to meet regularly in Santo Domingo in the spring of 1963. One, the Spanish-speaking Grupo Santa

A meeting place in Dominican Republic

Mercedes, grows from two to 18 members by the end of the year. G.S.O. New York lists as the contact person Abe F., who is also one of two men in the second group, for English speakers; this group, however, will last for only two years.

1963–64

Twelve Concepts for World Service published

In 1962, the General Service Conference accepts Bill's long-awaited manuscript for *Twelve Concepts for World Service*. In the introduction, Bill writes that his aim is

> "...to record the 'why' of our service structure in such a fashion that the highly valuable experience of the past, and the lessons we have drawn from that experience, can never be forgotten or lost."

"King-Size Sharing"

So reads the headline for the lead story in a 1964 edition of *A.A. Exchange Bulletin*. More than 100 large-scale A.A. conferences and conventions are being held around the world this year, dramatically illustrating the Fellowship's reach and growth. National conventions include those in Ireland, Australia, and England. In North America, states and provinces hold annual regional meetings—one being the Southeastern Conference, which draws members from 13 states. Among the conventions now held annually are those for International Doctors in A.A and International Conference of Young People in A.A.

A prison group Down Under

A.A. groups in prisons had spread across the U.S. from 1942 onward and had also begun meeting in Canada, Ireland, and Finland.

In 1958, Australia's first "group behind walls" is formed—the Magpie Prison Group at Fremantle Prison (right) in the port city of Fremantle, Western Australia.

Start-ups in Sri Lanka

A Loner in the former Ceylon had been listed with G.S.O. New York since 1959, but not until 1964 is the first A.A. group in the country formed. Its site is the capital city of Colombo, where a second group takes shape a year later. In 1976, by which time A.A. has spread to other Sri Lankan locales, a group in the Colombo suburb of Kotahena will mark its third anniversary with the publication of a booklet (right).

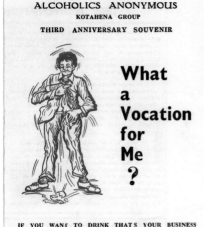

Anniversaries in Northern Europe

Belgium, by 1963 home to 18 A.A. groups in eight cities and towns, issues invitations (right) to its tenth anniversary celebration. Also marking its tenth anniversary is A.A. in Germany, with 26 groups in 14 cities and towns.

Overseas growth accelerates

An increase in the Fellowship's global service activity—including advisory correspondence from General Service Boards, the establishment of new literature centers, and more effective communication of A.A. Traditions—spurs the rapid growth of Alcoholics Anonymous around the world. By the end of the Fellowship's third decade, meetings are taking place in some 7,000 groups in 70 countries, with membership estimated at approximately 200,000.

1965—1984

A million members and growing

Alcoholics Anonymous begins its fourth decade on firm footing, garnering respect far and wide. Over the next 20 years, cooperation and sponsorship among A.A. countries will grow, the Fellowship's international conventions will expand in size and spirit, and the language of the heart will be spoken in at least 40 different tongues.

Joining the fold...

Bahrain	Iran	Nigeria
Bolivia	Israel	Paraguay
Cambodia	Italy	Poland
Canary	Kenya	Thailand
Islands	Luxembourg	Uganda
Ecuador	Malaysia	United Arab
Egypt	Malta	Emirates
Ghana	Marshall	U.S. Virgin
Guyana	Islands	Islands
Hong Kong	Nepal	Uruguay
Hungary	Niger	Vietnam

Hiker in Pakistan, c. 1965

Ten thousand-plus in Toronto

In July, more than 10,000 members from around the world meet in Toronto for the 30th Anniversary International Convention. Some 250 members of A.A., Al-Anon, or Alateen, plus 24 internationally known nonalcoholic authorities on alcoholism, are featured speakers at 69 jam-packed sessions. As the convention ends, attendees clasp hands and recite the Declaration of Responsibility, led by Bill and Lois. The convention program and souvenir book are shown at right.

19 65–66

Beginnings in Bolivia

While an A.A. group in La Paz, Bolivia, was listed with G.S.O. New York in 1965, little is known of its origins. Better documented are the two men considered A.A.'s Bolivian pioneers: Oscar G. and Jorge L., who meet in the city of Santa Cruz in 1971. After three years, Oscar will become a Loner when Jorge leaves for a job in La Paz. With a local woman named Dorita, Jorge forms an all-new group in La Paz, planting the seed for the eventual start-up of groups in Cochabamba and again in Santa Cruz. In 1987, the Cochabama group will host the first national meeting of A.A.s from across Bolivia.

San Francisco Cathedral, La Paz

Three start-ups in Ecuador

After a group of physicians from the Ecuadorean city of Cueca observe A.A. groups in neighboring Colombia, they are instrumental in getting a local group off the ground: Grupo Alianza Amiga, listed with G.S.O. New York in March, 1966. The second group takes shape when Eduardo A., who had achieved sobriety through A.A. in Washington, DC, returns home to Guayaquil and arranges with a local priest to hold meetings in his church. In the fall of 1971, the Guayaquil group helps Paulina M., who had gotten sober in Coral Gables, Florida, and Javier J., a businessman from Lima, Peru, to launch the first group in the capital city of Quito.

A.A. in a Communist country

The August/September edition of *A.A. Exchange Bulletin* reports that on June 30, 1966, "692 new A.A. Groups had been started in the past year—including one in a Communist country [unidentified], believed to be the first behind the iron curtain."

The Trustees' new alignment

In a move that stresses the Fellowship's full acceptance of responsibility for conducting its own affairs, the 1966 General Service Conference recommends and accepts a new alcoholic-to-nonalcoholic ratio of Trustees on the General Service Board. With the addition of U.S. and Canadian Trustees-at-large, the Board's membership is now made up of 14 alcoholics and seven nonalcoholics.

Loners and groups in Vietnam

As war rages in Vietnam, 10 American soldiers are listed as Loners by G.S.O. New York by 1966. In 1967, soldiers' groups number 11. By 1971, groups in Saigon, Long Binh, Cam Ranh Bay, and other locations keep in touch through SEA SIDE (SEA standing for South East Asia), a bulletin started by M/Sgt. Andie A. In a letter to G.S.O. New York, soldier Frank writes from the battle lines: "For years I prayed for sobriety, but now I pray the Serenity Prayer… God bless you."

Supply helicopter in Vietnam

A bulletin changes names

In the 1966 Holiday issue, the name of *A.A. Exchange Bulletin* (subtitled "News and Notes from the General Service Office of A.A.") is changed to *Box 4-5-9*, after the G.S.O.'s post office box at New York's Grand Central Station. In 1968, the journal will go tri-lingual with the launching of French and Spanish editions.

A.A. literature in Africa

The Literature Distribution Center in Johannesburg assumes the responsibility of furnishing complimentary literature from G.S.O. New York to new groups and Loners in South Africa. The material is in six languages: Afrikaans, English, German, Sotho, Xhosa (right), and Zulu.

ISIXHOSA

ALCOHOLICS ANONYMOUS

ABAZILI-TYWALA i "A.A."

Switzerland: the message in three languages

The year 1967 sees the creation of Switzerland's first General Service Office, when the Gremium (German for "committee") begins serving German-speaking A.A.s. The country's first group was French-speaking, however, taking shape in 1956 when an alcoholic in Geneva learned of Alcoholics Anonymous at a lecture given by an author of a self-help book, obtained A.A. literature, and arranged a meeting with friends. The first German-speaking group was launched in 1963 in Lucerne. The first Italian-speaking group will be formed in the canton of Tessin in 1974, and in 1979 a G.S.O. serving French and Italian Switzerland will open in Geneva.

Geneva and Lake Léman

Bill's writings printed and bound

The A.A. Way of Life, a collection of Bill's writings, is published as a daily source of comfort and inspiration. The title of the book will be changed in 1971 to *As Bill Sees It*.

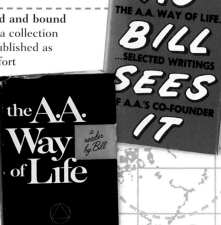

19 67–69

An international award from the Franciscans

In April, Alcoholics Anonymous receives the International Award of the Conventional Franciscan Fathers and Brothers. Dr. John L. Norris, chairman of the Board of Trustees, accepts the plaque and citation, which notes, in part,

> "the sympathetic understanding and the patient application of charity toward those afflicted with the disease of alcoholism has brought about the rehabilitation of thousands of alcoholics formerly thought to be hopeless alcoholics."

Meeting over the airwaves

Ben L., an Internationalist aboard the S.S. *Hudson*, writes to *Box 4-5-9* to report on A.A.'s first known ham radio group. "We have about 10 regular members," he writes, "and it's just like any other meeting." The group brings together members around the world every 24 hours. "Some nights, only a few and other nights the whole gang shows up," he continues. "More new men show up from time to time, and it is a thrill to hear a new signal breaking in."

HAM RADIO GROUP

First triennial survey in U.S. and Canada

At the 28th International Congress on Alcohol and Alcoholism, held in late summer 1968 in Washington, D.C., A.A. chairman Dr. John L. Norris reports on the findings of the first survey of members from all states and provinces. Sixty percent of the 11,355 men and women who responded at 466 meetings in 1968 reported that they had gone without a drink for a year or more. The survey, which will be taken every three years, also finds that 41 percent of members said they had not drunk alcohol since their first A.A. meeting.

The First World Service Meeting

For the first time, representatives from countries where A.A.s have established a G.S.O or a literature distribution center convene to share information on service structures, group services, publishing, and finance. The date is October 8-11, 1969, and the place is New York City. Attending are Bill W., Chairman Dr. John L. Norris, G.S.O. New York manager Bob H., and delegates from Australia, Belgium, Canada, Colombia, Costa Rica, Finland, France, Germany, Guatemala, Holland, Mexico, New Zealand, Norway, South Africa, United Kingdom, and the U.S.

Hungary's first open meeting

Midge M., a staff member of G.S.O. New York, travels to Budapest in June 1969 to attend a conference held by the International Institute on Prevention and Treatment of Alcoholism. While there, she arranges Hungary's first open A.A. meeting. Members Peter B. of the Netherlands, Inge L. (West Germany), Richard P. (Ireland), and Cecily C. (U.S.) address a group of Hungarian alcoholics as Archer Tongue, director of the Institute, translates. While a small group will be formed in Budapest in 1972, A.A. won't become firmly established in Hungary until the late 1980s.

Bridge over the Danube, Budapest

Growth of Spanish-speaking groups

As of 1969, 1,500 Spanish-speaking groups are listed at G.S.O. New York. A report states that there are probably many more, as evidenced by the knowledge that 14 groups in Buenos Aires are active but only two have sought to register.

Progress in Mexico

The five Spanish-speaking groups in Mexico City form an Intergroup Office and decide to hold semi-annual national conferences for all Mexican groups. A general services plan along North American lines is approved in September 1969. Shown at right is an ivory illuminated box depicting the Last Supper, a gift to Bill W. from a group in Yucatan. The inscription, in English, reads, "Thanks be to God for getting Bill sober so he could bring us a new world."

Loners gather in Malaysia

In February 1971, Enos C., an A.A. Loner working in Kuala Lumpur, places a notice in *The Malay Mail* newspaper seeking other Loners interested in holding meetings. Six weeks later, Enos reports to G.S.O. New York that with the addition of two Canadian A.A.s in Kuala Lumpur, the fledgling Pertama Group already numbers five. By the end of the decade, four more groups will have started in Sarawak and other Malaysian cities.

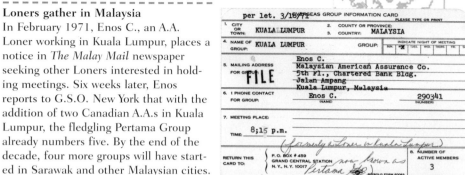

V.A. salutes A.A.

In a letter to the chairman of the Board of Trustees, the United States Veteran's Association congratulates Alcoholics Anonymous on its 35th anniversary and declares that the V.A. looks forward to continued "productive relationships with the numerous A.A. members who meet with alcoholics in our hospitals."

Hospital and prison groups worldwide

A G.S.O. New York report of the 1970 World Service Meeting notes that 54,031 "institution members" belong to the Fellowship worldwide: 20,160 in 742 hospital groups and 33,871 in 895 prison groups.

1970–72

Unity in Miami

Miami is the site of the Fellowship's fifth International Convention, the keynote of which is the Declaration of Unity:

> "This we owe to A.A.'s future: To place our common welfare first; to keep our Fellowship united. For on A.A. unity depend our lives, and the lives of those to come."

Attending are 11,000 people from 50 states and 27 countries—as reported by *Box 4-5-9*, "the biggest assemblage of alcoholics the world has ever seen—all of them sober!" The convention marks Bill W.'s last public appearance at an A.A. gathering.

A new home for G.S.O. New York

The G.S.O. takes an 11-year lease on new quarters at 468 Park Avenue South in New York City, gaining more space and saving rent money in the process. The office occupies the entire sixth floor.

The death of Bill W.
At the age of 75, Bill W. dies on January 21, 1971 at the Miami Heart Institute in Miami Beach, Florida. On February 14, groups around the world hold memorial meetings honoring Bill's work as co-founder of Alcoholics Anonymous, author of the Big Book and other publications, and chief architect and articulator of the Fellowship's principles.

Bangkok's first meetings
In Bangkok in 1971, two Americans of Irish descent—Jim L., a businessman with three years of sobriety, and Evelyn K., wife of a civil engineer under contract in Bangkok—team up to form an A.A. group. The next year they are joined by Jack B., a Redemptorist priest. In 1973, the three move their meetings from Evelyn's apartment to the Holy Redeemer Rectory and welcome new member Joanne—the wife of an American Embassy official— and George, a German-born U.S. military member. The stabilization of the Bangkok group soon gives rise to the founding of A.A. groups in Ubon and other Thai cities.

Royal Palace, Bangkok

Italy comes aboard
The start-up of A.A. in Italy is said to be 1972, when a small group of Americans meeting in Rome is joined by locals Giovanni and Ermanno. Assisted by some of the Americans, the two men soon join with Carol C. to form the first Italian-speaking A.A. group. Two years later, a group will be founded in Florence, and Milan will follow suit in 1976. In 1978, representatives of several groups meet to start negotiations with G.S.O. New York for the sponsorship of the publication of *Il Grande Libro* (the Big Book), which is already being translated into Italian. They succeed, and *Alcolisti Anonimi* (above) is published in 1980.

Lois's round-the-world trip
In an echo of their 1950 visit to Europe, Lois W. sets out on a nine-week trip around the world a year after Bill's death. Her traveling companion is Evelyn C., an early volunteer at the Al-Anon Clearing House and later a staff member at the Al-Anon W.S.O. During their journey the women meet with members of A.A. and Al-Anon in South Africa, Australia, New Zealand, Hong Kong, Tokyo, and Honolulu. (Shown below is a gift later presented to Lois, the Serenity Prayer in Japanese.) In *Lois Remembers*, Lois will write that "Seeing and feeling the loving devotion and oneness of A.A. and Al-Anon around the world did much to submerge in an overwhelming sea of gratitude my sense of personal loss."

A wealth of publications

A 1973 catalog of literature published by A.A. World Services lists and describes six books, five directories and handbooks, and dozens of pamphlets: 17 on A.A. recovery, 11 on unity and service, 15 on public information activity, and six directed to professional and business people. In addition to English, the literature is available in one or more of 19 languages.

Musings from members

Came to Believe, a 120-page booklet published by A.A., is a collection of stories by members who tell in their own words what significance the phrase "spiritual awakening" holds for them. Writes one,

> "I began to see another part of me emerging—a grateful me, expecting nothing, but sure that another power was beginning to guide me, counsel me, and direct my ways."

Poland's first steps

A group of alcoholics who have been meeting with physicians and therapists since the mid-1960s in the city of Poznan decide in 1974 to meet on their own and follow the principles of A.A. (Earlier meetings were organized by therapist Maria Grabowska, who had tried to have the Twelve Traditions and Twelve Steps published in Polish newspapers but was thwarted by the censorship office.) Led by Rajmund F., a Pole who became sober in 1973 and was fluent enough in English and German to translate A.A. literature, the group takes the name Eleusis, after the ancient Greek city the Roman Emperors favored as sanctuary. Growth accelerates, and by June 1985 almost 100 groups will be meeting across the country. The decorative plate shown above was presented to G.S.O. New York by grateful Polish members.

1973–75

Intergroups in Wales

The first group in Wales was founded in Abergavenny in 1963. Until then most alcoholics who wanted to attend A.A. meetings had to cross the border into England. A decade later, the Welsh Borders Intergroup is founded to link groups on both sides of the border (shown at right are the towns where the groups meet). An intergroup has also been established in South Wales—the Cymraig Intergroup, composed of groups in Cardiff, Swansea, Llanelli, and Newport.

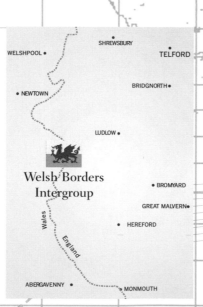

Welsh Borders Intergroup

SHREWSBURY
WELSHPOOL
TELFORD
NEWTOWN
BRIDGNORTH
LUDLOW
BROMYARD
GREAT MALVERN
HEREFORD
Wales
England
ABERGAVENNY
MONMOUTH

A fruitful relationship

By cooperating with Alcohol Safety Action Programs (A.S.A.P.), a number of A.A. groups not only carry the message to alcoholics but also contribute to safety. In conjunction with the judicial system, A.S.A.P. manages court cases for people charged with DWI and other alcohol-related offenses while educating and monitoring the offenders. A.S.A.P. refers many offenders to A.A. meetings.

Delegates descend on Denver
"Let It Begin With Me" is the theme of the Fellowship's 40th Anniversary International Convention, held in Denver, Colorado. Some 19,500 attendees stream into the city, and Host Committee members register arrivals at the rate of 400 per hour. At the formal opening session, a replica of the Big Book that gives new meaning to the word "big" dominates the dais: It is 28 feet tall.

A vote in Uruguay
Pablo L., an actor, undergoes detoxification at Montevideo's Clinica del Prado in 1966, is given a copy of the Big Book, and in turn seeks out an A.A. group to join. The closest is in Buenos Aires, where he frequents A.A. meetings during an extended stay. Returning home, he visits hospitals to carry the message. He then founds ADEA (for Amigos del Enfermo Alcoholico, or friends of the alcoholic patient), where alcoholics and their families share experiences. While some aspects of the A.A. program are used, others—including anonymity—are rejected. After A.A. Argentina urges ADEA to follow all A.A. Traditions and to take the Fellowship's name, the issue is put to a vote. The ayes have it, and on March 18, 1974, the first Uruguayan meeting of A.A. is held in Montevideo.

Downtown Montevideo

A new beginning in Portugal

English-speaking groups in Portugal had met as early as 1956 in Lisbon and 1959 at Lajes Air Force Base in the nearby Azores. Yet A.A. doesn't take root in the country until 1975, when expatriate American Ed A. returns from rehabilitation in the United States and begins spreading the A.A. message in hospitals. As a result, Portuguese-speaking groups are founded in Lisbon, Oporto, and Algarve. Aiding the growth and stability of the groups is Portuguese-language A.A. literature sent by A.A. Brazil.

Fast-forward in Iceland

Though the Reykjavik Group had been meeting in Iceland since 1954, a breakthrough occurs in the early 1970s, when a government-sponsored program begins flying alcoholics to the U.S. for help on a regular basis. Almost invariably they return eager to carry the A.A. message, leading to the 1976 publication of the Big Book in Icelandic. The subsequent explosive growth in membership results in a change in public opinion regarding alcoholism and the establishment of new treatment centers.

A.A. Archives open at General Service Office

In November 1975, Lois W. and Tom S. of Jacksonville, Florida (a former Trustee who chairs the archives at-large committee), cut a blue ribbon to officially open the A.A. Archives at G.S.O. New York. In a brief speech, Dr. John L. Norris points out that A.A. must continually renew itself by going back to its source, recalling Bill W.'s frequent request that the Board and G.S.O. "should put everything they do on the record." The archivist is nonalcoholic Nell Wing (right), who served as Bill's secretary for many years and is described as a "one-woman walking encyclopedia of A.A. lore."

A.A. in Jerusalem

With the aid of Canadian A.A. members who are part of the UN forces in the Middle East, the Shalom Group is formed in Jerusalem in 1975. The next year, member Jay S. reports to G.S.O. New York that twice-weekly A.A. meetings are being held in Tel Aviv as well as Jerusalem, in both English and Hebrew. The Shalom Group will also host a two-day convention to celebrate the first anniversary of A.A. in Israel. Shown above right are A.A. pamphlets in Hebrew and Arabic.

JUNAAB created in Brazil

While records show A.A. meetings were held in Brazil as early as 1947, the country's first General Service Board—Junta Nacional de Alcoólicos Anônimos, or JUNAAB—is created in February 1976. The establishment of a central office in Sao Paulo is spurred by local A.A. members' consultation with G.S.O. New York about translating the Big Book into Portuguese and publishing it.

A.A. meeting place in Brasilia

Third edition of Big Book published

Thirteen new stories appear in the Third Edition of *Alcoholics Anonymous*. By the summer of 1976, more than 1,450,000 copies of the Big Book's first two editions have been distributed worldwide, and both a Braille edition and audio tapes have been released.

19*76–79*

Membership tops a million

At the opening of the 26th annual meeting of the General Service Conference, held in New York in April 1976, new figures for the Fellowship's worldwide reach are reported: an estimated 28,000 groups in 92 countries, with membership totaling more than

1,000,000.

A younger Fellowship

An A.A. survey conducted in 1977 shows that over the previous three years the proportion of young members (those under 30) in the U.S. and Canada has jumped 50 percent and now accounts for almost 20 percent of North American membership. Surveys done by A.A. in Argentina, Colombia, El Salvador, Finland, France, Mexico, New Zealand, the United Kingdom, and West Germany yield similar results.

Early meetings in Cambodia

In the wake of the 1975 capture of the Cambodian capital of Phnom Penh by the Khmer Rouge, thousands of Cambodians fill refugee camps along the Thai border. In one camp, a U.S. aid worker whose brother is an A.A. back in New York recognizes that alcoholism affects many of the refugees, leading her to order and translate A.A. publications. Though up to 60 people attend daily gatherings based on A.A. principles, they cease when the camp closes. Some 15 years later, A.A. reappears in Cambodia when a few expatriates start a group in Phnom Penh. A.A. Australia responds to a request for sponsorship and also helps members to establish Khmer-speaking groups.

A milestone for the Grapevine

With the March 1978 issue, the circulation of the Fellowship's "meeting in print" reaches 100,000. In June 1944, copies of the periodical's first edition had numbered 1,200 and had gone out to 165 subscribers and other members of A.A. In 1983, selected A.A. Grapevine articles will become available on audio tape.

The first zonal meeting

Born of an idea set forth at the 1978 World Service Meeting, the first zonal service meeting—during which countries share experiences, strengthen unity, and offer help to A.A.s where service structures have yet to be set up—takes place in Bogota, Colombia in 1979. Delegates from ten Latin American countries convene in what is called the Ibero-American Service Meeting. Later, this biannual meeting will be called REDELA, a shortened form of Réunion de Las Americas (Meeting of the Americas). Zonal meetings will be launched in Europe in 1981, Asia/Oceania in 1995, and Sub-Saharan Africa in 2003.

Intergroup Office in Medillin, Colombia

A.A.'s first film

In the fall of 1979, the first public information film produced by the Fellowship—the 28-minute *Alcoholics Anonymous: An Inside View*—is released to A.A. service entities in the U.S. and Canada, enabling groups to provide it to television stations for airing. A panoramic view of sober living in A.A., the film shows a cross section of members in various settings—at work, at home, and at A.A. get-togethers and meetings.

Groups for the deaf

By the spring of 1979, G.S.O. New York has listed seven A.A. groups for people who are deaf. Also listed is an international deaf group whose members communicate by mail. *Box 4-5-9* reports that the use of non-A.A. interpreters, when necessary, "gives rise to the confidentiality question," but experience has shown that goodwill on both sides usually puts the issue to rest.

"I . . ."   *". . . am responsible."*

Celebrating New Orleans-style

In New Orleans, the sounds of jazz welcome some 22,500 paid attendees as they arrive at the Superdome on July 3, 1980—the first evening of the 45th Anniversary International Convention. A procession of nations, with A.A. members from around the globe carrying their national flags, is the prelude to two days of workshops, a three-day alkathon (round-the-clock meeting) at the Marriott Hotel, and the appearance at the Sunday morning Spiritual Meeting of Lois W. and "Smitty," the son of the late Dr. Bob.

1980–84

A famous article reappears

Forty-two years after Jack Alexander's "Alcoholics Anonymous" appeared in the March 1, 1941 *Saturday Evening Post,* giving the Fellowship national exposure, the magazine serializes the article in three editions. The editors decided it was time to reissue the article when they received a letter from a man whose father had gotten sober in 1942 after reading the story. In the meantime, A.A. had made its own effort to keep article alive with its pamphlet "The Jack Alexander Article About A.A.," first distributed in 1981.

Milestones in Malta

In Malta in 1983, the first translations of basic A.A. literature are approved and a Maltese-born member of A.A. Malta attends the bi-annual European Service Meeting for the first time. (Seventeen years prior, in 1966, an Irish veterinary surgeon living in suburban Valletta had listed the Malta Group—originally English-speaking, and later known as the International Group—with G.S.O. New York. In 1981, its Maltese members founded a Maltese Group in the Valleta suburb of Floriana.) Another significant event takes place in 1984, when Maltese women start attending meetings, making it easier for A.A. Malta to reach out to women struggling with alcoholism. Two other milestones will be reached in 1986: the opening of a General Service Committee and founding of a group on Gozo, Malta's sister isle.

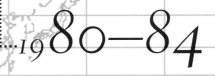

A biography of Dr. Bob

A biography of A.A. co-founder Dr. Bob, titled *Dr. Bob and the Good Oldtimers,* is published in time for the International Convention in New Orleans. The 382-page book combines Dr. Bob's life story with recollections of A.A.'s exhilarating and tumultuous early days in Akron and the Midwest.

"Pass It On" published

After five years of preparation, A.A. World Services publishes *"Pass It On": The Story of Bill W. and How the A.A. Message Reached the World.* In 25 chapters the book recounts, as described on the book jacket, "…the dramatic story of the founding of Alcoholics Anonymous, its early struggles and amazing growth." Among the photographs is one showing a newspaper report of an Oxford Group meeting in Akron (right).

1985—2004

A message without borders

Fortuitously for A.A., two world-changing events coincide as the 20th Century draws to a close. The dawn of the Electronic Age facilitates communication between A.A. offices and, in turn, country-to-country sponsorship, while the transformation of governments in Eastern European countries allows A.A.s to meet openly.

Joining the fold...

American Samoa	Czech Republic	Russia
Antarctica	Estonia	Saipan
Belarus	Indonesia	Saudi Arabia
Benin	Kyrgyszstan	Slovakia
Botswana	Latvia	Slovenia
Bulgaria	Lesotho	Tahiti
Cameroon	Lithuania	Togo
Chad	Malawi	Tonga
China	Moldava	Ukraine
Cook Islands	Monaco	Vanuatu
Croatia	Mongolia	Western Samoa
Cuba	Namibia	Yugoslavia
Cyprus	Romania	

Capetown, South Africa c. 1985

The Spanish Services Desk

Full-time Spanish Services at G.S.O. New York enters its second year. Up to the time it is absorbed by the Group Services Desk, the assigned staff member will help handle all correspondence in Spanish, translate pamphlets and bulletins, develop new service materials, and perform other services as needed. The drawing at right was sent to the G.S.O. by Berny, a Costa Rican member of A.A. "Hello!," it reads. "My name is The Happy Tico [Costa Rican] [and] I'm an alcoholic."

1985–87

A.A.'s golden anniversary

The Fellowship's 50th Anniversary International Convention in Montreal draws more than 45,000 members of A.A., Al-Anon, and family and friends—more than twice the attendance of the record-setting 1980 convention in New Orleans. Delegates from 54 nations give the gathering a truly international feel, and meetings in the Olympic Park Stadium are simultaneously translated into French, Spanish, and German. One of the honored guests is Ruth Hock Crecelius (a nonalcoholic), who is presented with the five millionth copy of the Big Book, the original manuscript of which she had typed almost half a century earlier when she was Bill W.'s secretary at their small office in Newark, New Jersey.

Traveling exhibits

The Cooperation With the Professional Community (CPC) committee reports that traveling exhibits of A.A. literature—which since 1956 have facilitated cooperation between the Fellowship and physicians, clergy, educators, and other professionals—are responsible for approximately 2,900 requests each year for literature and 2,500 requests for *About A.A.*, a newsletter for professionals. In the mid-1980s, displays large and small are used at no fewer than 26 national professional conventions and conferences per year.

Dr. Bob's house opens in Akron

The Akron house where Dr. Bob and his wife lived and raised their children—855 Ardmore Avenue—is opened to visitors in 1985. Much of the furniture is original (as is the still-working refrigerator, which Dr. Bob and Anne bought in 1934), and many of Dr. Bob's books line the shelves.

WSM revisits Latin America

Delegates from 25 countries with an A.A. service structure or office gather in Guatemala City, Guatemala, for the Ninth World Service Meeting (WSM). The 1986 meeting marks the fourth time the WSM has been held outside of New York, and the second in Latin America. Previous WSM hosts were England, Finland, and Mexico. The Mexican meeting place shown at right is one of tens of thousands in Latin America.

The journey in pictures

An updated version of *What Happened to Joe…and His Drinking Problem* (top) is released in 1985. A.A.'s first comics-style publication (it dates from 1967), traces the descent of a happily married construction worker into alcoholism and his eventual recovery through A.A. Another update of the comic (bottom) will be released in early 2004. A companion volume (*It Happened to Alice…*) is directed at women.

India's first G.S.O. conference

A.A. India holds its first General Service Office conference in Bombay (now Mumbai) in May 1987. By the year 2000, more than 20 conferences and P.I. (public information) meetings will have been held in different parts of India and the country's G.S.O. will have published the Big Book in eight languages: English, Hindi (as in the emblem shown above), Marathi, Tamil, Malayalam, Kannada, Punjabi, and Bengali. In the Delhi meeting room shown above hang banners printed with the Twelve Traditions— one in Hindi, the other in English.

Growth of electronic meetings

As the Fellowship expands rapidly around the world, some A.A. members turn to their personal computers to give and receive the message of recovery. Since the mid-1980s, electronic communication has been an updated and expanded version of the "telephone therapy" of A.A.'s earlier days. Bulletin boards set up on home computers are linked through national and international networks, enabling local users to join instant "meetings" with A.A.s all over the world. A number of international networks are listed with G.S.O. New York.

U.S.-Russia exchange bears fruit

Exchange visits between representatives of Russia's Temperance Promotion Society and Alcoholics Anonymous take place in 1987–89—part of the American-Soviet Dialogue on Common Problems sponsored by the National Council of World Affairs. By 1989, three A.A. groups are meeting in Russia—one in Moscow and two in Leningrad. Growth in Russia will proceed at a rapid pace, with at least 270 groups meeting in more than 100 cities by 2002.

Entrance to A.A.'s Russian-American Center, Moscow

The Language of the Heart published

An anthology of more than 150 Grapevine articles written by Bill W., *The Language of the Heart* documents the trial and error that resulted in A.A.'s spiritual principles of Recovery, Unity, and Service and articulates Bill's vision of what the Fellowship could become. For more than three decades Bill had often used the magazine as a vehicle for communication with members and groups.

1988–90

Baltic State start-ups

June 1988 sees the founding of Lithuania's first group, which meets in the Vilnius apartment of Romas O. (Romas had set foot on the road to sobriety when he read a Lithuanian translation of the Big Book in the fall of 1987.) In late 1988, Romas and fellow group members visit Riga, Latvia, and correspond regularly with that city's first group, founded by Pëteris and Austris in November 1988. By 2004, 110 groups will be meeting in Lithuania and close to 40 in Latvia. A.A.s will begin meeting in neighboring Estonia in 1989, in Tallinn.

The Big Book at 50

The golden anniversary of the publication of *Alcoholics Anonymous* is marked at the A.A. General Service Conference held in April 1989. The "birthday cake" baked for the

occasion (right) sports replicas of the covers of the First and Third Editions of the book, of which more than eight million copies have been sold or distributed by 1989. Fittingly, the 20 million sales mark will be passed in the year 2000.

A.A. in North Africa

Lou V., an A.A. in Cairo, writes in the June 1990 Grapevine that meetings have been held in Egypt since 1979, but that for the previous seven years A.A. countrywide membership had not grown above 20 or so. He says that most A.A.s

Egyptian meeting place, Cairo

are North American or European, and about a fifth are Egyptians who speak some English. In the northwest corner of the African continent, small A.A. groups in the Moroccan cities of Meknes, Rabat, and Tiznit have been active since the mid-1980s.

Two new tools

Local Bridging the Gap (or "temporary contact") programs, which help newcomers make the transition from treatment centers to attending A.A. meetings, gain momentum. (Bridging the Gap differs from temporary sponsorship by simply facilitating the introduction of new members to meetings in the outside world.) In addition, the quarterly *Treatment Facilities Newsletter*—designed to help members who carry the message into hospitals and halfway houses—is mailed to chairpersons of A.A. treatment facilities and chairpersons of hospitals and institutions committees.

Bursting at the seams in Seattle

Some 48,000 people converge in Seattle for the Fellowship's Ninth International Convention, far exceeding the anticipated head count. The theme is "Fifty-five Years–One Day at a Time." More than 250 standing-room-only meetings are held at Seattle Center and around town—at the time, the largest convention ever hosted in Washington's largest city.

A first for Turkey

The first nationwide gathering for Turkish A.A.s is held at a hotel in Kizil Eahaman, nestled in the pine-covered mountains 100 kilometers outside the capital, Ankara. Twenty-four delegates from groups in Ankara, Istanbul, Izmir, and Adana communicate in both Turkish and English during three days of meetings and activities.

Johanna S., of the Ankara International Group, reports to The Grapevine that the event was "a gathering of active, intense, happy, recovering alcoholics who met, dined, walked, and enjoyed each other's company. We touched each other's lives." The sketch above accompanied an account of the event in The Grapevine.

A meeting in Minsk

In November 1990, a few dozen A.A.s from Latvia, Lithuania, and Ukraine gather with their counterparts in Minsk, Belorussia (now Republic of Belarus) to coordinate the services in their respective countries. In April 1991, a second conference will be held in Riga, Latvia, attracting 180 A.A.s from the same four countries plus Russia.

Romania: Two steps to success

In 1988, Fran P., an American A.A. teaching English at Romania's University of Timisoara, attempts to start a group with the help of Rodica, an alcoholic student—but the program's reliance on a Higher Power runs afoul of government authorities. Only in 1991, almost two years after the Communist government has fallen, will an A.A. group flourish in Timisoara. In 1993, Petrica and Damian, alcoholics hospitalized in Bucharest, will start a group in the capital city with the help of Dr. Doina Constantinescu and Patricia and Lee, an A.A. couple from the U.S. The flyer shown below is typical of A.A. Romania's efforts to reach out to struggling alcoholics.

A.A. General Service Office moves uptown

After 20 years on Park Avenue South, on Manhattan's East Side, G.S.O. New York relocates to the Interchurch Center at 475 Riverside Drive, home to dozens of non-profit organizations. The date is March 1992. (Serendipitously, the 19-story limestone building was built by the Rockefeller family, so important to the Fellowship's early history.) The G.S.O. occupies the entire 11th floor, with The Grapevine offices one flight down. Every year, hundreds of A.A. members from around the world visit. A tour of the offices and Archives is provided on the spot.

1991–93

Canadians cross language barriers

In an effort to carry the message to the Native North American population in the Northwest Territory, who speak seven different languages, A.A.s in the Yellowknife area go about gathering all known Native American translations of A.A. literature. They confirm the translations' accuracy and build files that are easily accessible to A.A. members. The efforts continue, paving the way for an Eastern Canada regional trustee and a fellow A.A. to travel to remote communities in northern Quebec in May 2004, distributing A.A. literature in the Inuktitut language to educators, prison officials, attorneys, and mayors.

Movement in Southeast Asia

In 1991, around five A.A.s begin to meet in Ubud, Indonesia, auguring the start-ups of small groups in Kuta, Sanur, and Seminyak. The meetings are attended by expatriates and tourists passing through, but by 2003 some 40 Indonesians will have joined A.A. The early 1990s find stable groups of expatriates or native speakers meeting in Thailand, Vietnam, Singapore, and Malaysia.

Missives to the Persian Gulf

After military action begins in the Persian Gulf in 1991, the G.S.O. New York staff member on the Loners/International Desk hears from scores of A.A.s serving in Saudi Arabia. Each is sent a copy of the new book *Daily Reflections*, a free subscription to the Grapevine, and any A.A. literature that is requested. One letter, from Sgt. John L., is representative. In it, he writes,

"A lot of good has come out of my being in this desert. I've finally been forced to really take a good look at my life. As the Big Book says, I'm 'building an arch to walk through a free man [sic].'"

First Native American Convention

"Living Our Traditions Through Sobriety" is both the purpose of Native American A.A. gatherings and the motto on the emblem they create (below) for the first annual convention for Native American A.A.s from the U.S. and Canada. Among the 800 attendees at the event, held in October 1991 in Las Vegas, are Native Americans from some 100 tribes plus representatives of tribal alcohol programs, halfway houses, and treatment centers. In ensuing years, Washington, South Dakota, North Carolina, and other states hold their own conventions as well, and in 2004 the fourteenth National/International Native American Convention will convene in Minneapolis.

European Service Meetings

In Frankfurt (above), 32 A.A. delegates from 18 countries attend the 1991 European Service Meeting (ESM), the zonal conference that has been held biannually in the German city since 1981. The ESM gives delegates from European groups the opportunity to present progress reports and share their respective countrys' problems in the hope of finding solutions.

Mexico-Cuba sponsorship

In a textbook example of country-to-country sponsorship, Mexico succeeds in getting Cuba's first group going in February 1993: Grupo Sueño (Dream Group), in Havana. The year before, Cubans Ciro V. and Juan A. had asked government officials for permission to provide information about A.A.—in their words, "a program without nationalities, a political agenda, or financial interests"—but without success. Once A.A Mexico informs the Cuban government of the particulars of A.A.'s program of recovery, the government changes its mind and welcomes the Fellowship. By the end of 2004, some 200 groups will have become active in Cuba. The arrival of A.A. in the country is celebrated every January, as shown in the poster below.

"Special needs" committees

A number of A.A. groups worldwide form committees to make the Fellowship accessible to any alcoholic with special needs, including those who are visually or hearing impaired, bedridden, wheelchair bound, or suffering from learning disorders. Among the tools employed are Braille editions or audiotapes of A.A. literature and videotapes of the Big Book in American Sign Language.

戒酒無名會

Planting a seed in China

In 1995, retired Chinese physician Dr. Lawrence Luan, who owns a primary health care clinic in Santa Barbara, California, asks the clinic's administrator, who happens to be an A.A. member, to accompany him on a medical business trip to his hometown of Daiwan. To be granted a visa, the administrator must speak on a health topic, and while Chinese authorities request that he address HIV/AIDS, Dr. Luan arranges for him to speak to five doctors at the mental hospital in Daiwan on his subject of choice: alcoholism. The speech is well received, as are Chinese-language copies of the Big Book he presents to the doctors. In 1998, he will share his experience at the Pacific Regional Forum in Sacramento as a member of the International Panel. As a result, a member of the San Francisco Intergroup begins organizing a "messengers" group that will travel to China. Shown above is "Alcoholics Anonymous" in Chinese script.

1994–96

Canada's golden anniversary

During the first weekend of July 1995, more than 6,000 A.A.s and friends from Canada, the U.S., South America, Europe, and Asia gather in Toronto at the Metro Convention Center to celebrate 50 years of Alcoholics Anonymous in Canada. The program includes 34 speaker meetings, 26 panels, 40 marathon meetings, and two talkathons.

Celebrating 60 years

The theme of the 60th Anniversary International Convention—"A.A. Everywhere–Anywhere"—is borne out as nearly 56,000 people from the U.S., Canada, and 85 other countries gather in San Diego, California, in June-July 1995. Among the highlights are an opening-night waterfront dance with fireworks exploding across the bay, an opening meeting that sees Jack Murphy Stadium filled to capacity, and oldtimers recounting stories at the "Forty Years or More Sober" meeting, Saturday night's featured event. Shown at right is the convention's souvenir book.

AA EVERYWHERE–ANYWHERE

A Family Album and Souvenir of the International AA Convention, San Diego, Calif. June 29-July 2, 1995 – 60 years.

First Asia/Oceania Service Meeting

Years after Bob P. of New Zealand conceives the idea of a zonal meeting serving Asian and Pacific Island A.A groups, the first Asia/Oceania Service Meeting (AOSM) is held in Tokyo in March 1995. Bob P. chairs the meeting, which with its "Twelve-Stepping Your Neighbor Country" theme emphasizes the shared responsibility of carrying the message in this part of the world. Attending are delegates from Australia, Hong Kong, Japan, Korea, New Zealand, and Vanuatu.

香港

5th

ASIA-OCEANIA SERVICE MEETING OF ALCOHOLICS ANONYMOUS
City Garden Hotel, Hong Kong
July 6 – 8, 2003
"The Three Legacies – Recovery, Unity, Service"

Se publica La Viña

A Spanish-language edition of The Grapevine arrives in the summer of 1996. In the new bimonthly magazine *La Viña*, articles translated from The Grapevine share space with original material written in Spanish. *La Viña* is distributed in North America, Latin America, and Spain, and in ensuing years is welcomed by Spanish-speaking A.A.s worldwide.

1997—2000

www.aa.org

After approval by the General Service Board, G.S.O New York launches a site on the World Wide Web on December 22, 1995. With a click, users can now instantaneously access information about the Fellowship in English, Spanish, and French. In spring 1998, G.S.O. New York will share the experience of computer-savvy A.A.s when it issues a list of Frequently Asked Questions for A.A. entities looking to set up their own Web sites. In 2000, "aa.org" will undergo a major expansion.

A Japanese General Service Board

In Tokyo, a General Service Board composed of eight trustees, including two nonalcoholics, starts operating in January 1996. At the time, an estimated 3,500 to 4,000 members are meeting in 290 groups. Japanese A.A. members visit and support Korean groups and vice versa, and in the early years of the new century A.A. Japan will join with G.S.O. New York to sponsor emerging groups in Mongolia. The handmade card at right, presented by the Kansai district office to a G.S.O. New York staff member visiting Japan, reads "Willingness, honesty, and open-mindedness are the essentials of recovery."

Support for French Equatorial Africa

A.A. France's sponsorship of African countries begins with a contact between Jean-Yves M. and a Loner from Cameroon, Donatien B., chief warden of a prison and an alcoholic. He achieves sobriety with Jean-Yves's help and determines to carry the message.

Jean-Yves and Jean-François L. travel to Cameroon in 1997 and are surprised to find that Donatien has started a prison group that has grown to 54 members. During his stay, Jean-Yves meets with officials, police directors, and members of the clergy. Yearly trips to Africa by A.A. France from 1998 through 2001 will facilitate the launching of groups in Benin, Chad, and Togo. Above, Cameroon villagers greet a visitor from G.S.O. New York with the customary singing and dancing as his traveling companion (foreground), an A.A. from the Douala group, joins in.

A.A. takes root in China

Four visitors from China—psychiatrist Guo Song and physicians Li Bing, Wang Qing Mei, and Guizhen Liu—attend the 2000 A.A. International Convention in Minneapolis as observers. G.S.O. New York subsequently sends letters and A.A. literature to the four and soon learns of the formation of two groups: one started by Guo Song at the Treatment Center of Beijing's Anding Hospital, the other by Li Bing with her patients. In August 2001, two G.S.O. New York staff members and Dr. George Vaillant (a Class A trustee) travel to China. They meet with medical practitioners and attend meetings of Beijing's two A.A. groups and one in Changchun—at this point, the three Chinese-speaking groups existing in China. By invitation, Dr. Vaillant addresses a gathering of some 50 physicians on the subject of alcoholism.

Greeting the millennium in Minneapolis

Some 47,000 people celebrate freedom from the bondage of alcoholism at the eleventh International Convention, held in Minneapolis, Minnesota, in the summer of 2000. The theme is "Pass It On–Into the 21st Century." A memorable event is Walk-the-Walk, when a stream of attendees from 86 nations walks the blue line laid down from the Convention Center to the Hubert H. Humphrey Metrodome on their way to the opening ceremony.

Al-Anon's first international convention

Forty-three years after its founding, Al-Anon holds its first international convention. The time is July 1998, and the place is Salt Lake City, Utah. As the century draws to an end, 24,000 Al-Anon and 2,300 Alateen groups are meeting in more than 110 countries.

Membership tops two million

As the new millennium begins, A.A.'s worldwide membership is estimated at

2,160,013.

Another membership milestone in the year 2000 is the number of groups, which for the first time surpasses the 100,000 mark.

Pole to Pole

Even alcoholics in the most farflung parts of the world—the Arctic Circle and Antarctica—have received the Fellowship's message by the year 2000. With the support of Canadian groups, A.A.s meet in Baffin Island and other far-north locales, while members posted to McMurdo Air Force Base in Antarctica organize meetings for military personnel and others who come and go.

BOX 4|5|9

...e of A.A.

VOL. 46, No. 3/ JUNE-JULY 2000

A North American milestone

In spring 2000, the 50th General Service Conference is held in New York City. Delegates from 92 A.A. regions and areas in the U.S. and Canada, trustees, directors and G.S.O. and Grapevine staff members listen to reports and inspect finances, just as their counterparts had done half a century before. One activity is a tour of the new General Service Office in Manhattan's Morningside Heights neighborhood.

Sponsorship Down Under

A.A. Australia, active since 1945, helps A.A.s in Phnom Penh, Cambodia, establish Khmer-speaking groups. The country's service office also assists in the establishment of groups in East Timor, New Guinea, and other Pacific locales. The service office in neighboring New Zealand—which for years has translated A.A. literature into Maori (see Serenity Prayer at right), Fijian, Samoan, and other Pacific island languages—launches an initiative to carry the message to correctional facilities in 32 countries in Oceania and the Pacific Rim.

Te Inoi Mauri Tau A Te AA

Ē Te Atua tukuna mai ki au te mauri tau
Ki te tango i nga mea e kore e taea e au te whakarereke
Tukuna mai te ngākau māia
Ki te whakarereke i ngā mea
Ka taea e au, ā,
Tukuna mai hoki te mātauranga
Kia mohio au ko tehea tehea

First woman chairs General Service Board

In 2001, a woman is elected to chair the General Service Board for the first time: Elaine McDowell (right), who had served as a Class A (nonalcoholic) Trustee for nine years. As chairperson, Dr. McDowell brings more than 28 years of experience in the prevention and treatment fields and an abiding faith in A.A.'s basic principles.

20OI—O4

A.A. at Ground Zero

In the wake of the attack on the World Trade Center in New York, exhausted A.A. members among the firefighters, police, and clean-up crews realize the need for A.A. meetings near Ground Zero. At the same time, a Red Cross official reports to G.S.O. New York that many requests for A.A. meetings have been received. The organization then assigns to A.A. a room in a Red Cross respite center just southwest of the site, its door bearing a circle and triangle. To accomodate everyone, a second room just north is provided. A.A. meetings are organized by Southeastern New York Area 49 and New York Intergroup, and the rooms become places where A.A.s can not only meet but also rest, talk, and meditate. Members crafted the iron plaque shown above and presented it to G.S.O. New York and the Intergroup of A.A. as a memento.

The Big Book's Fourth Edition

In November 2001, a new edition of the Big Book—the culmination of four years of development and 25-plus committee meetings—rolls off the presses. While the first 164 pages remain unchanged, the new edition includes the stories of 41 sober alcoholics (24 new and 17 "keepers" from the third edition) reaching a wider cross-section of membership by reflecting the breadth of A.A. experiences, ages, beliefs, and ethnicities.

A meeting in Poland

A.A.s from 13 countries travel to Warsaw, Poland in April 2002 for an Eastern European Service Meeting (EESM). Joining delegates from Belarus, Bulgaria, Czech Republic, Estonia, Hungary, Kyrgyzstan, Latvia, Lithuania, Moldova, Poland, Russia, Romania, Slovakia, and Ukraine are guests from Germany and Finland. The meeting is meant as a bridge to World Service Meetings for countries that do not yet participate in them. Since the early 1980s, A.A. Germany had sponsored groups in former East Germany and in Czechoslovakia and Hungary, while Finland has provided much support for Russia. In many countries, membership will continue to surge—particularly in Poland and Russia, which in 2004 will have 1,700 and 300 groups respectively. The card above is a reproduction of one of the artworks created by an A.A. member in Warsaw.

Progress in Sub-Saharan Africa

In June 2003, the first Sub-Saharan Africa Service Meeting is held at the Willow Park Conference Centre (right) near Johannesburg, South Africa. Present are two delegates each from Botswana, Kenya, Lesotho, Malawi, Namibia, South Africa, Tanzania, Uganda, and Zimbabwe, along with representatives from the General Service Offices of Great Britain and U.S./Canada. This zonal meeting is part of the Into Africa initiative, launched by A.A. South Africa in 2000 to improve cooperation with professionals and overcome the problem of A.A. literature distribution in a region with more than 250 languages. A delegate later reports that "Saturday night's family style dinner was filled with laughter and sharing as we expressed our joy in a long day of intense work."

Pacific Island groups

From Saipan and other Micronesian islands to Tahiti and elsewhere in French Polynesia, the A.A. message spreads to all corners of the Pacific Ocean. In the Philippines, the Big Book has been translated into Tagalog and Cebuano; in Vanuatu, meetings are conducted in English, French, and Bislama (the native tongue). By the end of 2004, groups that have been active at one time or another include those in American Samoa, the Cook Islands, Fiji, Guam, the Marshall Islands, Tonga, and Western Samoa.

Meeting place on Rori Namur, Marshall Islands

Success in Latin America

Country-to-country sponsorship, prolific publishing of A.A. literature by Central and South American General Service Offices, and the biannual REDELA help to carry the Fellowship's message to virtually every country in Latin America. As of 2004, Mexico has some 13,280 groups, Brazil 4,680. Among Latin American countries with 200 or more groups are Argentina (850), Venezuela (280) Uruguay (248), and Cuba (200); those with 100-plus groups include Chile (147) and Peru (140). In 2003, the REDELA is held in Maracaibo, Venezuela (see poster at right), the thirteenth such meeting since 1979.

Stepping Stones made State Historic Site

Acting on a recommendation from the New York State Board of Historic Preservation, the governor signs a declaration making Stepping Stones, the Bedford Hills house Bill and Lois called home from 1941, a New York State Historic Site. Bill wrote at Wit's End (his separate uphill study, above), and an upstairs nook in the house itself became the first office for Al-Anon Family Groups.

Quick growth in Mongolia

The first national convention of A.A. in Mongolia (July 2004) is the result of six years of work. It began when a nonalcoholic physician, Dr. Erdenebager, became interested in A.A. and urged meetings outside of those in treatment facilities in Ulaan Baator. Then, in 1999, two newly sober A.A.s and a physician traveled to Moscow to find ways to make A.A. work in Mongolia. When G.S.O. New York received a request from members for literature in the native language, A.A. World Services aided in the publication of the Big Book in Mongolian (2002). The 25 groups meeting in Mongolia in 2003, by then with the sponsorship of A.A. Japan, jump to 41 in a year. The mountainside structure above is a Buddhist Temple whose monks, friendly to A.A.s efforts, were visited by a G.S.O. staff member.

A new digital archive

Sixty years-worth of Grapevine content becomes available online when the A.A. Grapevine Digital Archive is launched on July 1, 2004. Subscribers are able to access some 12,000 stories, thousands of letters, A.A. history in the making—and, yes, countless cartoons and jokes. By selecting Digital Archive on the home page of www.aagrapevine.org, subscribers are able to search for topic by magazine department, theme, date, or keyword.

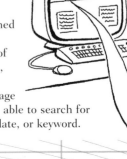

Index

• A.A. members cited for their role in group start-ups or other endeavors are further identified by country.

• Boldface page numbers indicate a photograph of a person, place, or publication.

I am responsible… • Yo soy responsable… • Je suis responsable…

나는 책임이 있읍나다… • Ke na le maikarabelo… • Saya bertanggung jawab…

Jeg er ansvarlig • Ik ben verantwoordelijk, • ‏...אני אחראי‎

Minulla on vastuu • Ich bin verantwortlich… • JESTEM ODPOWIEDZIALNY

Ég er ábyrgur... • Io sono responsabile... • ....مسؤول ابا

JEG ER ANSVARLIG… • Eu sou responsável… • ลันรู้จักรัยพิดชอย …

Oku ou fatangia'aki • Ben sorumluyum… • Juqondene Nami

I AM RESPONSIBLE...

WHEN ANYONE,
REACHES
I WANT THE H
ALWAYS TO BE
AND FOR THAT:
I AM RESI